Mask and Sword

Modern Asian Literature Series

Mask and Sword

Two Plays for the Contemporary
Japanese Theater by Yamazaki Masakazu

translated by J. Thomas Rimer

Columbia University Press
New York   1980

The Japan Foundation, through a special grant, has assisted
the Press in publishing this volume.

Library of Congress Cataloging in Publication Data

Yamazaki, Masakazu, 1934–
  Mask and sword.

  (Modern Asian literature series)
  Translation of Zeami and Sanetomo shuppan.
  1. Zeami, 1363–1443—Drama. 2. Minamoto, Sanetomo,
1192–1219—Drama. I. Yamazaki, Masakazu, 1934–
Sanetomo shuppan. English. 1980. II. Title.
III. Series.
PL865.A57Z2813   895.6′2′5   79-26162
ISBN 0-231-04932-3

Columbia University Press
New York   Guildford, Surrey

In memory of two remarkable artists, Zeami Motokiyo and Minamoto Sanetomo, with the thought that their own restless spirits might be amused, at least, to find themselves described in a language of which they never heard.

Contents

Illustrations follow page 24 and page 120.

Introduction

Thanks to the efforts of many gifted and dedicated translators and scholars, the literary accomplishments of the traditional Japanese theater—*nō*, *kyōgen*, and *kabuki*—are well established. Less attention, however, has been given to the drama of *shingeki*, the modern theater in Japan. Plays of merit, composed in what might be termed the international style, have been written and performed successfully in Japan since the beginning of the century, when the work of Ibsen came to have a powerful impact on a generation of young Japanese playwrights, just as it did on a similar generation throughout Europe and the United States. The movement to create a drama sensitive to contemporary concerns suffered many vicissitudes in Japan, but by the postwar years, the form had become one thoroughly adapted to the needs of writers, actors, and audiences alike.

In terms of dramatic construction, such modern plays are composed in a fashion familiar to Western audiences. Serious postwar Japanese playwrights are as interested in philosophy and psychology as are their European counterparts and, on the surface, contemporary Japanese dramaturgy seems to owe as much to Ionesco, Pirandello, Beckett, and Albee as it does to any older Japanese theatrical form. Nevertheless, the concerns of playwrights like Mr. Yamazaki are very much rooted in Japanese culture, a culture which, in its contemporary manifestations, raises in countless ways particular issues of great potential significance for the drama, in particular those dealing with personal and national identity. For a Western

[1]

reader, the significance of such plays as the two translated here goes beyond the texts themselves. Both *Zeami* and *Sanetomo* stand as mirrors, reflecting their author's attempt to grasp the nature and significance of his own society. Using the past as a means to gain perspective on the present represents, in these two dramas, the author's central methodology.[1]

Among those playwrights of serious literary ambition working today, Yamazaki Masakazu (born 1934) deserves special pride of place. His interests are wide-ranging and his knowledge of Japanese and Western theatrical history profound. Educated at Kyoto University and at the Yale Drama School, Mr. Yamazaki now divides his time between his writing for the theater, his teaching career (he is currently in charge of a new program on the history of world theater at Osaka University), and his work as a literary critic and philosopher of aesthetics. Perhaps Mr. Yamazaki might best be termed an intellectual who expresses himself through the drama; and like others in this category, his work shows a philosophical ambition and a power of language not usually evidenced in plays written for the commercial theater in any country. Some additional details concerning his career are contained in the interview included as an appendix to the translations and will be of interest to those who would like to know more of the general state of contemporary Japanese theater.

In choosing his subject matter from historical sources, Mr. Yamazaki has taken two of the most powerful figures in traditional Japanese culture. Both Zeami Motokiyo (1364–1443) and Minamoto Sanetomo (1192–1219) represent, for different reasons, what might be termed "modal personalities," that is, personalities who serve as models, positive or nega-

---

1 Many of Yamazaki's plays, of course, do not use historical themes. One of his plays with a purely contemporary setting, *The Boat is a Sailboat* (1973), is available in translation in Ted Takaya, ed., *Modern Japanese Drama, an Anthology* (New York: Columbia University Press, 1979), pp. 137–202.

live, for later generations. Such figures seem to exemplify crucial, basic attitudes and so continue to fascinate men at other times, assuming occasionally metahistorical status. Philip Rieff, the intellectual historian, has written that such personalities in effect define the nature of their culture and, indeed, seem to change as their culture changes, since successive generations redefine such modal personalities in terms of their own preoccupations and concerns.[2] Rieff has chosen Freud as the modal type of personality for the twentieth century in the Western world and has gone on to suggest that, in any culture, it is the perceived personality, not the abstract idea, that remains the crucial element. "In culture," he writes, "it is always the example that survives; the person is the essential idea."[3] Sanetomo and Zeami occupy precisely such roles in Japanese culture. The two men stand as forceful personalities about whom each generation has found it necessary to take a stand. Yamazaki's view represents one contemporary position, but there have been others before, and there will doubtless be others to follow.

Zeami, undoubtedly the greatest genius in the history of the Japanese theater, was a child actor in the touring troupe of his father when, in 1374, his performances were seen in Kyoto by Ashikaga Yoshimitsu (1358–1408), the Shōgun and legendary patron of the arts. Yoshimitsu took in the young actor and his father's troupe, arranged for the boy to have a superior education, and supported the company until his death thirty-four years later. Brought into the court atmosphere, Zeami, through his activities as an actor and playwright, lifted the *nō* drama to great heights of expressiveness and profundity. Later in his life, after the death of Yoshimitsu, Zeami fell from favor and, in the midst of various personal difficulties, wrote a number of secret treatises on various aspects of the art of *nō* that represent some of the most practical and most philosophic writing on the art of the

2 Philip Rieff, *The Triumph of the Therapeutic* (New York: Harper and Row, 1966), p.2.
3 *Ibid.*, p. 31.

theater produced in any civilization. Zeami was a man totally dedicated to his art, and it is this particular aspect of his career that Mr. Yamazaki has reconstructed, in a poetic fashion, in his play. Many of the facts of Zeami's life are known as a matter of course to a well-educated contemporary Japanese audience.

In the case of Minamoto Sanetomo, the historical situations involved are more complicated, and some knowledge of the period will help clarify a Western reader's perceptions of the play. The turbulent period in which *Sanetomo* takes place is as familiar, and as important, to the Japanese as our own Civil War era is to us; therefore the playwright can assume that his Japanese audiences will already posssess a certain amount of historical background before they come to the drama itself.

The great civil war that climaxed in the battles of 1185 destroyed the power of the Heian court in Kyoto and resulted in the creation of a military government, ruled by the Shōgun, in the northern port city of Kamakura. The result was a shift in the balance of power between civil and military forces that was by no means resolved during the lifetime of Sanetomo himself. Indeed, Sanetomo's death on the steps of the Hachiman Shrine in Kamakura remains one of the most celebrated political assassinations in Japanese history, as any present-day visitor to the site will quickly learn.

Sanetomo's father, Minamoto Yoritomo, was the victor in the 1185 battles, and he consolidated his power in Kamakura in order to escape the influence of the Kyoto court, whose role he hoped to reduce to a merely ceremonial function. In order to gain ascendancy, Yoritomo used family ties: his wife Masako was from the powerful Hōjō family, which was strong in northern Japan. Yoritomo became the first Shōgun of Kamakura, and at his death the title was passed on to his first son Minamoto Yoriie. The real power, however, was taken by Yoritomo's wife Masako and her powerful brother Hōjō Yoshitoki. Yoriie was eventually removed from his position, exiled, and evidently murdered at the behest of his mother and uncle. Sanetomo, the younger brother of Yoriie, was next given the position of Shōgun when he was a mere child of eleven. With his father a Minamoto and his mother a Hōjō, Sanetomo had intimate connections with the two most powerful factions in the country, a fact that may have made his own quest for self-definition all the more difficult. Sanetomo was, among other things, an accomplished poet, and his teachers included some of the greatest literary figures of his age. Sanetomo's own collection of *waka*, or 31-syllable poems, called the *Kinkaishū* is still available in modern annotated editions, and the playwright has quoted several of Sanetomo's remarkable poems in the text of his play. Sanetomo also had plans to build a ship to sail to China, and the historical facts as presented in the play are quite accurate in terms of the actual accounts that remain.

Yet, however carefully wrought the historical dimensions of these two plays may be, the author's concerns are strikingly contemporary. In the case of *Zeami*, Mr. Yamazaki seems intent on using his chief character as a trenchant example of the tension between a total dedication to art and the human pressures of society, family, and the familiar world. In the play, Zeami stands as a kind of secular priest, ready to abandon every human compromise, even those that seem in his best interests, for what he takes to be the dictates of his art. The battle between Zeami's sense of self and his sense of vocation provides the means to lift the play to a powerful, abstract level in which the argument, defined and redefined through a colorfully theatrical series of encounters, sustains the dramatic tension. The play is thus not merely "about" Zeami himself but about larger, philosophical issues, and thus it succeeds where other plays about dramatists (dramas about Shakespeare, for example) often fail. Yamazaki seeks not to define Zeami so much as to explore the real nature of the possibility of the art he represents.

In the case of *Sanetomo*, the world of art (here poetry)

plays some role in Sanetomo's quest for self-definition, but the world of politics looms much larger, thus putting more of a burden on the reader unfamiliar with the complex relationships between the historical characters concerned. Mr. Yamazaki was quick to ascertain certain parallels in Western literature: Sanetomo, whose father is dead and whose mother is in league with conflicting forces, becomes in the play very much like Hamlet in his relations with his mother Gertrude and his uncle Claudius, who resembles in certain ways Masako's brother Yoshitoki. Mr. Yamazaki does not imitate Shakespeare, but he does make a number of ironic and poetic references to *Hamlet* that, for a Japanese audience, are both astute and audacious. For a Western reader, such references may work in a reverse fashion, making a familiar story serve as a lens through which to look at the complex political world the playwright has put on the stage in *Sanetomo*. The helpful metaphor works both ways.

While *Zeami*, a rich and romantic play, is constructed along fairly simple and chronological lines, the dramaturgy of *Sanetomo* is considerably more complex, involving a group of modern actors who begin rehearsing but soon "become" the ghosts of the historical figures in the play. These ghosts in turn reenact a kind of psychodrama concerning their relations to Sanetomo, in order to understand who and what he may have been. The text of *Sanetomo*, in comparison with that of *Zeami*, is more restrained, darker, and, in the original, surprisingly witty. Much of this wit springs from the ironic juxtaposition, for a Japanese audience, of the popular modern notion of the character of Sanetomo against the image created by the playwright. To a certain degree, this level of comprehension must remain missing for foreign readers, since we lack the background to savor the full flavor of certain scenes. There are examples of similar plays in our own tradition: the same kind of ironic juxtaposition can be seen in Ionesco's 1972 *MacBett*, in which Shakespeare's *Macbeth* is recast along the lines of the modern playwright's concerns.

Introduction

Despite possible difficulties imposed by such historical elements, however, the plays hopefully convey some of their original power in translation. As Mr. Yamazaki makes clear in the interview, his fascination with the nature of human personality is very close to contemporary Western views. The fact that such shared concerns are, in the case of *Zeami* and *Sanetomo*, rooted in a different theatrical and historical tradition gives them a special piquancy and dramatic power.

The text of *Zeami* has been translated from the author's revised version of the text which appears in the *Shinchō bunko* series (Tokyo, 1974). The English text might be considered a reading version, rather than an acting version, of the play.

The text of *Sanetomo* (originally titled *Sanetomo shuppan*, or *Sanetomo Sets Sail*) is taken from the text as printed in the *Kakioroshi shinchō gekijō* series (Tokyo: Kinyōsha, 1973). As my translation of *Sanetomo* was originally prepared for an English language production, Mr. Yamazaki took the opportunity to make a number of changes, both to simplify certain historical details and to emphasize certain relationships between the characters for the benefit of foreign readers. Therefore the translation reproduced here differs on occasion from the original printed Japanese text. In addition, both translated texts have been read by the playwright Richard France and by Professor Robert Hapgood, who made useful suggestions concerning the spoken dialogue.

I would like to thank the Japan Foundation for considerable help with this project, both in bringing Mr. Yamazaki to St. Louis for the American premiere of *Sanetomo* in 1976, and for help in funding the translation and publication of this book. I would also like to thank Dr. Richard Palmer, Director of Edison Theatre at Washington University, whose interest in learning about modern Japanese theater led him to take a profound interest in directing *Sanetomo*, which he undertook with the cooperation of the playwright. The play was per-

[7]

formed as part of the regular season of the Edison Theatre. After the St. Louis performances, the troupe was invited to visit New York for a performance of *Sanetomo* at Japan House, thanks to the efforts of Mrs. Beate Gordon. Dr. William Danforth, Chancellor of Washington University, also took a personal interest in helping to fund the troupe's trip to New York. Mrs. Sachiko Morrell, of the Washington University East Asian Library, was most helpful to me in my attempts to locate historical and other information. Without all this assistance and the constant enthusiasm of Mr. Yamazaki himself, the production, and this book, would not have come into being.

I would also like to thank William Bernhardt of Columbia University Press for his encouragement, as well as my editor, Jennifer Crewe, for her fine work in editing the manuscript. And I would particularly like to thank Susan Messenger and Debra Jones, on the staff of Washington University, for their patient and skillful help with the preparation of the typed manuscript.

A final note: names throughout are given in the usual Japanese fashion, surnames first, personal names following.

J. Thomas Rimer
St. Louis, Missouri
January 1980

Zeami

Originally published in Japanese as *Zeami*.
(Tokyo: Kawadeshobō-shinsha)

First produced by the *Haiyūza* troupe in Tokyo in 1963, *Zeami* received the Kishida Prize as the best modern drama of the year. *Zeami* has also been performed in English (1965), in another translation by Kenneth Butler, and in Italian (1971).

Characters

ZEAMI
MOTOMASA, his eldest son
MOTOYOSHI, his younger son
TSUBAKI, his wife
ASHIKAGA YOSHIMITSU, the former Shōgun, now retired
ASHIKAGA YOSHIMOCHI, his eldest son
ASHIKAGA YOSHITSUGU, YOSHIMOCHI's half-brother
LADY KUZUNO, the mistress of YOSHIMITSU
HOSOKAWA, a government official
AKAMATSU, a government official
LORD SANJŌ, a court noble
LORD ŌE, a court noble
OLD SORCERESS
OLD BEGGAR
DANCING BEGGAR
BIRDCATCHER
HAGI, a dancing girl
KIKYŌ, HAGI's daughter
KAEDE, KIKYŌ's daughter
DŌAMI, ZEAMI's old teacher
ON'AMI, ZEAMI's nephew
NOBLEMEN
ATTENDANT
ENVOY, of the Shōgun
Government OFFICIAL
Various RETAINERS
IMPERIAL GUARD
DANCERS, both male and female
CHORUS
OUTCASTS

Act One

Time: The play covers a period of twenty-five years, from April 1408 through April 1432. Dates and events have occasionally been altered to suit the needs of the play. In Act One, ZEAMI *is forty years of age. At the end of the play, he is seventy.*

Place: Kyoto; the gardens of YOSHIMITSU'S *palace;* ZEAMI'S *home; the streets of Kyoto.*

The Fourth Month of 1408. The outer gardens of the place of ASHIKAGA YOSHIMITSU, *in the hills north of Kyoto. The architectural construction, however, should not seem realistic. A dividing wall in a checkered pattern of dark blue and white, and several glittering gold pillars will serve to create the proper scenic effect.*

There are several steps in the front of the stage, suggesting the entrance to an open, roofed corridor. The cherry trees are in full bloom. The light from the shining blossoms fills the stage, making the faces of the characters on stage seem somehow flushed. Toward stage right stands an ox cart, decorated in a wholly fabulous manner, motionless, its blinds drawn. Nearby stands a fierce-looking muscular warrior with a halberd in one hand, who will remain there until the close of the act.

As the curtain rises, there are three characters gathered together at stage left: the OLD SORCERESS, *the* OLD BEGGAR, *and a middle-aged* DANCING BEGGAR. *They have a frightening and mysterious appearance, of the sort of people who perform as a means to beg their living. At some distance from them sit close to one another a young* BIRDCATCHER, *and the dancing girl* HAGI.

[11]

OLD BEGGAR: Bloody. The wind has a bloody smell. There will be more death.

DANCING BEGGAR: The soldiers fight in the west. The farmers revolt in the east. No wonder everything smells of blood.

OLD BEGGAR: But now the breeze is blowing from within the palace.

DANCING BEGGAR: Still, the same bittersweet wind that blows the flowers can carry the smell of death as well.

OLD BEGGAR: As I think about it, I can see how the air of this palace in the mountains, so filled with flowers, might well be stifling with the odor of death. I wonder. Has the performance by Zeami for the Emperor finished yet?

DANCING BEGGAR: Just about now.

OLD BEGGAR: Who is here watching him today?

DANCING BEGGAR: No shortage of people suitable for death. The Emperor is there. And Ashikaga Yoshimitsu, ruler of the nation, with his son the Shōgun Lord Yoshimochi, and his younger brother Lord Yoshitsugu. And all their attendants.

OLD BEGGAR: Omit the Emperor. He's no more than a living corpse. That leaves the three Ashikaga, father and sons. Watching that special command performance, surely one of them can be counted among the dead.

DANCING BEGGAR: You're a sorceress, old woman. You're supposed to know these things. Who is going to die this time?

OLD BEGGAR: It's no use. You can't badger an old woman like her to tell you anything.

DANCING BEGGAR: Well then, let's make a bet on it, you and I. I think it is Yoshitsugu who cannot live. Because Lord Yoshimochi, thin and withered though he may be, is still the Shōgun. Why should he let his younger brother live? After all, Yoshitsugu was born of a different mother.

OLD BEGGAR: No, quite the contrary. Remember, Lord Yoshimitsu himself is very fond indeed of his younger son

[12]

Lord Yoshitsugu. And what exactly is the rank of Shōgun? Worthless, a floating thing.

DANCING BEGGAR: What will you stake on it?

OLD BEGGAR: I'll stake, I'll stake.

DANCING BEGGAR: What then?

OLD BEGGAR: How about this small medicine box? I found it on the body of a dead warrior, killed in that battle at Ōmi a while ago. And you?

DANCING BEGGAR: I'll stake this gold lacquer hairpin. Two days ago I helped break into a storehouse. I pulled it from the head of a nobleman's wife.

OLD BEGGAR: Good. I say Yoshimochi.

DANCING BEGGAR: And I say Yoshitsugu.

BIRDCATCHER: How bothersome you are. Murder—that's work for professionals. Not something for old fools like you to sit back and observe for your own amusement. (*Getting up.*) So, Hagi, Sing us a little song.

HAGI: There's no festival here now. No one will pay for my song. If I sing for you, what will you give me?

BIRDCATCHER: What would you like?

HAGI: You're a birdcatcher, aren't you? Catch me a nightingale.

BIRDCATCHER: What do you want to do with it? Eat it?

HAGI: I hate nightingales. They sing with so much joy. They interrupt me.

BIRDCATCHER: I'll catch you one then. I certainly don't want a nightingale to spoil your song. Now then, sing.

HAGI (*she sings; the effect is cold, rather than gloomy*):
All the brides, all the young girls
Never stop watching the dancers;
They know the men they like to watch,
They know them all,
They point their fingers—"That's the one!"
Shall I tell you how I feel?

(*Everyone sings the last line together, as a chorus.*)

[13]

(*The Birdcatcher picks up his pole and exits. The* OLD BEGGAR *and the* DANCING BEGGAR *clap their hands.*)

OLD BEGGAR: Isn't that the truth? And these days it's not just the children and the women who are on the lookout for something interesting. All the courtiers and warriors seem to have time for nothing but those plays.

DANCING BEGGAR: Today the performance is for the Emperor. Tomorrow there's a public performance. All this is a bit unusual, even for Lord Zeami. I wonder what makes people want to watch that kind of thing?

OLD BEGGAR: Because no one wants to look at himself. What a wretched world this is! Looking each other in the eye would be worse still. That's why they'd rather line up and stare at an illusion.

DANCING BEGGAR: As far as you're concerned, we serve as a rubbish heap for the world to take a glance at when there seems nothing better to do.

OLD BEGGAR: Of course. These respectable people only manage to forget themselves and lead their own lives because they can find us so pitiful.

DANCING BEGGAR: As far as we're concerned, I can agree with you. But what about Zeami? His renown is enormous.

OLD BEGGAR: If his work is something watched by other people, then it must be the same for him too.

DANCING BEGGAR: He is radiant. At the height of his powers. It is hard to think that he inhabits a rubbish heap.

OLD BEGGAR: Come to think of it, the Kanze family has certainly risen in the world. Do you know how his father Kan'ami made his living as a young man? He went around with his little plays from one shrine and temple to another. And his audience? Town shopkeepers and some farmers. And look what has happened, in one generation. Zeami, his son, is practically an object of worship.

[14]

DANCING BEGGAR: It was in the summer, when Zeami was only thirteen. He was a beautiful boy then, in close attendance upon Lord Yoshimitsu at the great Gion Festival at the capital. A glittering bloom. All the girls of Kyoto seemed to have eyes only for him.

OLD BEGGAR: And not just the women. The Shōgun, Lord Yoshimitsu, was more intent than anyone. After all, Zeami was talented. He was handsome. And Hagi. (*Coarsely.*) You know what they said. For service at night, there was no consort who could match Zeami.

HAGI: How disgusting. I don't want to hear anything about it.

DANCING BEGGAR (*laughing*): When it's a question of a young boy like that, what do you expect? But thanks to all that, the theater of Zeami has reached glorious heights. Then again, Zeami has certainly had his appeal for the high-ranking women of the land as well. Have you heard, Hagi? They say that Zeami has recently fallen in love with yet another.

HAGI: That shouldn't come as any surprise. Lord Zeami is always involved in romantic escapades.

DANCING BEGGAR: But this time the object of his affections holds a high rank indeed. If Zeami handles things badly this time he may well discover that the results will be fatal.

OLD BEGGAR: He only seems attracted to women of high rank.

HAGI: And he throws them right over. That seems to be his chief pleasure.

DANCING BEGGAR: Why Hagi! I think you find him attractive yourself! (*He laughs loudly.*)

(*The* BIRDCATCHER *returns. On the top of his pole is a nightingale he has pierced. In one hand he carries a sprig of cherry blossoms.*)

BIRDCATCHER: I've come back with a nightingale, just as you've asked. So now, sing another song for us.

[15]

HAGI: Very well. (*She pulls away the sprig of cherry blossoms, tears off a handful of the flowers, and throws them about as she sings.*)

I'm glad the nightingale is dead.
I'm glad the flowers fall.
Set fire to the universe itself!
I will dance, madly dance, alone!
No flowers! And no birds!
Shall I tell you how I feel?

DANCING BEAR: "Shall I tell you how I feel?" (*Laughing.*) What a frightening girl this is! Burn down the whole world, dance all by yourself! If you are as wilful as your song, you'll never get to Paradise.

HAGI (*rising*): Do you think Paradise can exist for an outcast like me? A street dancer who wanders around from place to place? In this world at least, I will go on showing myself, showing myself, until I dance myself to death. (*She strips off more flowers and scatters them about, dancing and singing, "I'm glad the nightingale is dead," etc. Suddenly a voice is heard.*)

VOICE: Make way! Make way for the Shōgun!

(*A group of* RETAINERS *enters and blocks off both sides of the staircase.* LORD HOSOKAWA *and* LORD AKAMATSU *enter with the Shōgun,* YOSHIMOCHI. *With the exception of* HAGI, *all the others fall silent.*)

HAGI: Watch me, everyone. I, Hagi, will dance, in the garden of this palace, before the procession of the Shōgun himself.

BIRDCATCHER: I'm watching. Dance, dance your wildest, Hagi.

HAGI (*with fierce gestures*):

Set fire to the universe itself!
I will dance, madly dance . . .

AKAMATSU (*signaling to an* ATTENDANT *as he cries out*): How dare you? Stop this at once! (*The* ATTENDANT *pushes her down.*)

[16]

BIRDCATCHER: What do you think you are doing?

AKAMATSU: It is outrageous that persons like yourselves should even come here. And how much worse to perform this disgraceful dance before the Shōgun himself.

YOSHIMOCHI (*to* HOSOKAWA): Who are these people?

HOSOKAWA: They call themselves "The People of the Seven Districts." They are outcasts, who deal in this sort of despicable dancing in order to earn their living.

YOSHIMOCHI: What are such people doing in my father's palace?

HOSOKAWA: I cannot imagine. Perhaps they represent some enthusiasm of Lord Akamatsu.

AKAMATSU: What an extraordinary idea. I am a man whose only interest is in military affairs. I haven't the slightest concern about these people.

HOSOKAWA: True enough. You slept through that beautiful performance of Zeami's just now.

YOSHIMOCHI (*to the* BIRDCATCHER): Tell me, who has permitted you to come in here?

BIRDCATCHER: My Lord, it was Lord Zeami who sent for us, saying he might have some need for us. When we explained this at the main gate, the guards went out of their way. Why they even bowed to us!

AKAMATSU: This one—he's like all of those entertainers now. Everyone behaves in this outrageous fashion. And all because Zeami has come to exert such an unreasonable influence. And all because, I'm sorry to say, your father Lord Yoshimitsu has been over-generous in his patronage.

HOSOKAWA: Perhaps, Lord Akamatsu, you should go and tell Lord Yoshimitsu your views directly.

AKAMATSU: It is only because I felt that Lord Yoshimochi would understand me that I spoke at all. These *nō* dramas used to be performed by outcasts in order to make their living. I really cannot understand why, in the case of

Zeami and his family, we warriors should extend such
support.

YOSHIMOCHI: Perhaps it is unfortunate. I admit that I too
have served as a protector, as a patron for Zōami.

AKAMATSU: No, things are different when a man knows his
place. Like Zōami. But look at Zeami. How many lords
have lost their rank, even their lives, for having failed to
flatter him—no matter what they might have felt in their
own hearts?

HOSOKAWA: Yet you have lavished gifts on Zeami yourself, I
believe.

AKAMATSU: Yes, before. But now my Lord Yochimochi is
Shōgun. Things are no longer the same.

(*Suddenly* YOSHITSUGU *approaches them from the rear.*)

YOSHITSUGU: So, Lord Akamatsu. Has my brother really taken
charge of things now?

YOSHIMOCHI: Yoshitsugu. Just what are you trying to say?

YOSHITSUGU: After all, our father is still in excellent health.
Indeed, he should live to a ripe old age.

YOSHIMOCHI: I am the Shōgun.

YOSHITSUGU: But who actually refers to you as the ruler? You
are the patron of Lord Akamatsu. Yet even he, when he
speaks of the ruler, means our father.

AKAMATSU: Lord Yoshitsugu, you must not misunder-
stand . . .

YOSHITSUGU: I realize that I only hold the rank of a retainer.
But my father's blood flows thicker in my own veins than
in my brother's. Why, in the first place, how can anyone
say my brother is my father's child, when he can't even
grasp the real nature of Zeami's art? True enough, Yoshimochi has purposely supported Zōami, if only to show
his independence of spirit. And how absurd that is.
There is nothing in the art of Zōami that can oppose the
genius of Zeami. And actually, who was it who took note

[18]

of Zōami's talents in the first place? Our father Yoshi-mitsu, of course. My brother may wish to oppose the views of my father, but only through the eyes of my father can he see anything at all. Lord Hosokawa, can't you see the irony in all this?

AKAMATSU: What about the art of these outcast performers here? Do you feel that what they do is anything different from Zeami?

YOSHITSUGU: The lotus flower sucks up the mud of the swamp to bloom. And you, who turn away from poor wretches like these, what can you understand of a performance by Zeami? Ah, look at that old woman there. Isn't that the old sorceress who always walks by the river? Let's get her to tell us our fortunes.

HOSOKAWA (*to* YOSHIMOCHI): This old woman is said to have surprising powers to predict the future.

YOSHIMOCHI: Old woman! Come here!

(*She approaches.*)

YOSHIMOCHI: Look at my face, old woman. Tell me what you see. Tell.

YOSHITSUGU: Don't worry about what you see. Tell us your prophecy. Tell.

OLD SORCERESS (*after a moment of silence*): Light is Darkness. And Darkness is Light.

YOSHIMOCHI: What's all this? Say it once more.

OLD SORCERESS: Light soon becomes Darkness. And Darkness soon becomes Light.

(*Everyone falls quiet.*)

YOSHIMOCHI: Lord Hosokawa, unravel this mystery for me.

HOSOKAWA: No. No, I . . . cannot.

YOSHITSUGU: Nevertheless, try your best.

HOSOKAWA (*with a stiff laugh*): Why take all this so seriously? Why put any credence in the foolish words of this old woman?

[19]

AKAMATSU (*coming forward*): I'll solve your riddle.

YOSHITSUGU: What a daring fellow you are, Akamatsu. Well then, proceed.

AKAMATSU: The Light represents your father, Lord Yoshimitsu. And, I regret to say, the Darkness is Lord Yoshimochi, your brother, the Shōgun. (*Drawing his sword.*) Thus, Light will soon turn to Darkness, while Darkness now turns to Light.

(*The* RETAINERS *draw their swords to protect* YOSHIMOCHI.)

YOSHITSUGU (*with a loud laugh*): So you think that's it? Our father represents the Light, and my older brother the Darkness? But perhaps my brother, the Shōgun, represents the Light, and I, Yoshitsugu, must stand for Darkness.

HOSOKAWA: My Lord. Those are words of rebellion.

YOSHITSUGU: Rebellion? I thought such words had lost their meaning since our family came to power. Well, Akamatsu?

YOSHIMOCHI: Old woman. I have something to ask you. Between Light and Darkness, there exists another realm— that of Shadow. Light and Darkness stand eternally opposed. Yet Shadow follows along with Light.

OLD SORCERESS: Yes. That is so.

YOSHIMOCHI: And he who lives in Shadow—when the Light has vanished, will he disappear as well?

OLD SORCERESS: It is as you say.

YOSHIMOCHI (*pointing out* YOSHITSUGU): That man there. Could he manage to pass for a man who lives in Shadow? (*He laughs.*)

OLD SORCERESS (*forcefully*): No. He is not such a man.

YOSHIMOCHI: He's not?

YOSHITSUGU: Your irony is rather heavy-handed. If I could become the Shadow of my father, I would be happy indeed.

OLD SORCERESS: He cannot. The heirs to the Shōgun may become Darkness, but they can never become Shadows.

[20]

YOSHITSUGU: Old Lady! Why should this be so?

OLD SORCERESS: You have not understood. It is not so much that Darkness hates the light. Rather, he who lives in the Shadow has no existence of his own. It is this that you do not understand.

YOSHIMOCHI: The Shadow must hate the Light. But no! That would be like strangling yourself with your own hands. Why? Why should the Shadow hate the Light? More than Darkness?

OLD SORCERESS: Because, sometimes, even Darkness may become Light. But a Shadow always remains a Shadow, a reflection that only continues, on and on.

YOSHIMOCHI: But what sort of person can become a Shadow? Can an outcast take on such a role?

OLD SORCERESS: No, it is not an easy thing to do. Most men may not. It is not an easy thing at all.

AKAMATSU: Why, who fits the part better than someone like Zeami? His origins are unknown. And he certainly is a man who lives in Shadow.

HOSOKAWA: Lord Akamatsu, I think you have said too much.

AKAMATSU: I don't care. What do you think of someone who makes his way in the world by selling his favors, then ends up by sharing our Lord's pillow? He is at best the Shadow of a man.

YOSHITSUGU: Still, Lord Akamatsu, Zeami has quite a reputation, and as a man. I hear that more than one or two girls of high birth—and married women too—have been quite intimate with him.

AKAMATSU: How perfectly outrageous. The upstart uses them, then throws them away like worn-out shoes.

YOSHITSUGU: Still, there's something that doesn't quite fit. A man so successful with women can hardly be called a Shadow.

AKAMATSU: It occurs to me that Zeami may be carrying on this way out of envy. Like a cripple who wants to triumph over ordinary men. He steals their wives, even though he doesn't really want them.

YOSHITSUGU: Well. You seem to know every dreary detail. Perhaps, Lord Akamatsu, I might ask you about the health of your own good wife . . .

(AKAMATSU *pulls furiously at his sword.*)

YOSHITSUGU: Put up your sword. I'm sure we'll be seeing each other on the battlefield. Tell me, old lady. Is Zeami really this Shadow that you spoke of?

(*She shakes her head broadly, from side to side.*)

YOSHITSUGU: I understand. But, sometime—could he become so?

OLD SORCERESS: Dreadful. A dreadful thing.

YOSHIMOCHI: You can make no prediction?

OLD SORCERESS: I might even predict the death of a person. But something as dreadful as this . . . (*She shakes her head.*)

(*They all look at each other.*)

YOSHIMOCHI: Well then, I must leave you, Yoshitsugu. And the next time we meet, I hope that Light will not have turned to Darkness.

YOSHITSUGU: My hope is the same.

(YOSHIMOCHI, AKAMATSU, *and* HOSOKAWA *leave the stage.*)

YOSHITSUGU (*lowering his voice*): You told me that Zeami had asked you to come. Do you know why?

DANCING BEGGAR: I do not know. Perhaps he needed our help for some little prank or other.

YOSHITSUGU: I see. The imperial performance is finished now. Zeami has no doubt gone to pay his respects to the Emperor. I will call him. You wait at the rear carriage entrance. Here, too many people can see you.

DANCING BEAR: Thank you. We are grateful.

YOSHITSUGU: There's one more thing. (*Lowering his voice.*) I know you must have good connections with all those packhorse drivers in Ōmi and Kōchi. Don't worry. I

[22]

know all about the whole thing. I know they don't just use their horses to haul freight. Any time there's any kind of uprising, there they are, leading on the farmers. Sometimes it seems they might have the power to take on all the military forces in the country. I've even heard that recently they've been giving aid to the forces of the rebellious Southern Court.

DANCING BEGGAR: Why no, we . . .

YOSHITSUGU: You have nothing to hide from me. (*He hands them money.*) Take this. Keep it. And, if something should ever come up, don't forget how Yoshitsugu asked for your support.

(*Voices are heard.* YOSHITSUGU *hurries off.* SANJŌ KINTADA, ŌE MOCHIFUSA, *and two* NOBLEMEN *enter.*)

SANJŌ: Whatever was said to him, I cannot imagine the Emperor having consented to watch a *nō* performance.

ŌE: You are perfectly safe in confiding any suspicions to me, but if you make a similar remark in certain quarters, you'll soon lose your head.

SANJŌ: The whole affair is humiliating. Don't you agree?

ŌE: The nobility has learned over these many years to take quite a number of humiliating things in stride. Why should Zeami pose any particular problem?

SANJŌ: We've long been resigned to envying the strong. There's nothing degrading about having to put up with robbers and bandits, on whatever scale. But we cannot permit ourselves to be humiliated by Beauty. Ordering the world through Beauty? Only the nobility has the right to do that.

ŌE: I understand what you say. Yet think what Zeami showed us today. Did he not truly reveal a noble beauty?

SANJŌ: Exactly. He has stolen the appearance of the nobility.

ŌE: By all means let him steal it. Beauty can only triumph when what it steals is our appearance.

SANJŌ: If only the form had been stolen, no harm would have

been done. Even if a little violet by the side of the road tries to put on airs like a nobleman, he'll not succeed in attracting attention. But Zeami has stolen something far more important from us. Our rank. There are many beauties. But among them, the ceremonies we perform are the most beautiful of all. And now these miserable, vulgar songs and dances stand in revolt against our rites. They will soon take the place of these ceremonies themselves. And the Emperor now seems prepared to accept that usurpation. From now on, the nobility is doomed to watch, spectators in a theater.

ŌE (*laughing*): Still, what's wrong with that? In this life, what better place is there, to sit and watch?

SANJŌ: Sitting in a theater. Nameless. Faceless. A horde of animals, kept so they can provide applause for the actors. We are no longer hated. We are no longer feared. The nobility has finally disappeared altogether.

ŌE: Tell me, Lord Ōe, you have surely heard of shadow puppets. When there is no light, you see nothing. But, tell me. Do you ever see the Light itself?

SANJŌ: Certainly not. All you see are the Shadows.

ŌE: Lord Sanjō. What we see so clearly before our own eyes— all these things are merely Shadows.

SANJŌ: Are you trying to tell me that Zeami is merely a Shadow? Then who represents the Light? Certainly not us. We are merely the spectators.

ŌE: Look at this. (*He takes from his robe a* nō *mask, carved to represent the face of a young girl.*) This mask was specially carved for me by Chigusasaemon himself. To many, this may seem a mask like any other. But not to me. In this wooden visage, I see the face of one particular young girl. A street girl to whom, thirty years ago, I actually pledged myself. To tell you frankly, I was completely infatuated with her. She was of low birth, but haughty beyond measure. She was light as a bird, artless as an

[24]

Zeami, Act One. Left, Zeami (Gabriel Walsh), right, Lady Kuzuno (Terri Lee Reed). 1965 New York production.

Zeami, Act One. Left, Zeami (Gabriel Walsh), right, Hagi (Anna Stanovich), with the beggars. 1965 New York production.

Zeami, Act One.
Lady Kuzuno
(Annamaria Guarieri).
1971
Italian production.

Courtesy of Yamazaki Masakazu

Zeami, Act One. Hagi (Gigi Reder), center, and the beggars.
1971 Italian production.

Zeami, Act Two. Left, Lord Ōe (Claudio Gora), right, Lord Sanjō (Marcello Bertini) 1971 Italian production.

Zeami, Act Three. Zeami (Senda Koreya). 1963 Tokyo production.

Courtesy of Yamazaki Masakazu

Zeami, Epilogue. Zeami (Senda Koreya).
1963 Tokyo production.

Courtesy of Yamazaki Masakazu

Zeami, Epilogue. Motoyoshi (Harada Kiyondo), center, and the dancers.
1963 Tokyo production.

angel I was trapped between two hot pokers—love and jealousy.

SANJŌ: What a surprising story.

ŌE: But then one day . . . after I had this mask made, I began to find myself more strongly drawn to the mask than to the real woman herself. At first the mask only served to divert me when I could not have her with me. Later, I began to love the mask, even when the girl was at my side. The mask seemed neither bright nor dim; yet somehow it was so much more beautiful than the living girl herself.

SANJŌ: What a cruel business.

ŌE: A curious rivalry developed in me between the real girl and the mask. Finally, the mask triumphed over the girl. I embraced the mask and forgot her. The Shadow murdered the living reality. Yes, perhaps you are right. Perhaps what I did was cruel. But my eyes. It was my eyes that won out. Lord Sanjō. Zeami is the same. He is the Shadow of us all—old man, young girl, courtier alike. And who gives life to the Shadow? The eyes of us, who look on.

SANJŌ: All very ingenious, but I'm not sure I agree. Putting the Light into the eyes of the spectators? A gloomy state of affairs indeed.

ŌE: Mankind arrives in those spectators' seats with a grudge against the world. And there, on the stage, the Shadows of that whole world are on display before us. So we take our revenge by attributing to them more life than they possess. In the end, from those same seats, we can triumph over all the vicissitudes of the world—in this case, my affair with that girl.

(ZEAMI *enters quietly, accompanied by* DŌAMI. ZEAMI *is in his mid-forties, a strong man of generous build.*)

SANJŌ: Do you mean, then, that Zeami has no real existence at all?

ŌE: He is a brilliant Shadow. But he is a Shadow without Light. Like this mask. If I don't look at it, it remains merely a piece of wood.

ZEAMI: Lord Ōe. Are you still on that subject?

ŌE: Oh! Lord Zeami. I'm a flute that blows only one note. So the subject remains the same. And I'm so pleased that you, more than all the others, understand what it is I am talking about.

ZEAMI: Do you feel comfortable in a spectator's seat, looking at the world?

ŌE: Ah! You haven't quite got the point yet, I think. Those seats are filled with nails. Hardly the sort of seats a happy man would choose.

ZEAMI: A man who lives in shadow can't quite follow all of that.

ŌE: Then I envy you.

ZEAMI: Do you really? But enough of this for now, Lord Ōe. I did want to tell you that I've devised something quite ingenious for you. Something I hope to show you quite soon.

ŌE: Something ingenious?

ZEAMI: Yes, and I hope you will find it enjoyable. As for my part, I will find it a pleasure to present it to you. But for the moment I am quite tired. I hope you will permit me to excuse myself.

ŌE: I appreciate your kindness. And I must say, Lord Zeami, that these days I find something of the marvellous in your performances, something that seems touched with the Holy.

ZEAMI: I am moved by your words. But it is beyond the powers of a mere Shadow to apprehend things in that fashion. Everything is due to you, my Lord of Light.

ŌE: No, rather to those wise eyes of Yoshimitsu, who first brought you to fame. And as long as those eyes continue to shine, your art will triumph. Goodbye then.

[26]

Zeami

(ŌE *and* SANJŌ *leave the stage.*)

DŌAMI: What happened to you, Fujiwaka? I thought your performance quite listless today.

ZEAMI: Please stop calling me Fujiwaka. I'm not a child any more. So don't call me by my childhood name.

DŌAMI: You know I can't help but think of you as a real child of mine. And especially now, when you seem troubled, I can't help but see you as that Fujiwaka of thirteen or fourteen.

ZEAMI: And I know too that when you start calling me Fujiwaka, some lecture is soon to follow. What is it today?

DŌAMI: But that's just what I wanted to ask you. Today was a unique moment in the whole history of our profession—the first time an Emperor has ever witnessed a performance of *nō*. Do you really think your performance was worthy of the occasion?

ZEAMI: Let me speak frankly. I felt no strength in my arms or legs. I admit my performance was a failure.

DŌAMI (*after a pause*): Tell me. What happened?

ZEAMI: There were deficiencies . . . in the spectators.

DŌAMI (*sputtering*): Well, so you think you've become so grand as all that! If the Buddha and all his saints came to watch the great Zeami, I suppose you'd find fault with them too! And for such a boastful performance as that, you would probably invite all the demons and devils to watch as well.

ZEAMI: Actually there were enough demons and devils at Yoshimitsu's palace today. Unfortunately, there was no angel to preside as Patroness of Art.

DŌAMI: You mean a woman.

ZEAMI: Yes, the one I yearned for was not seated with the others there among the blossoms.

DŌAMI: Yearned for . . . Who could that be? Have you gone and fallen in love with another princess?

ZEAMI: Are you concerned for me? Actually I feel apprehen-

[27]

sive myself. This time, I may be involved in an illicit affair that could well cost me my life.

DŌAMI: An illicit affair? Wait. There was one person who was missing today, the wife of . . .

(*The* BIRDCATCHER, HAGI, *the* OLD SORCERESS, *the* OLD BEGGAR, *and the* DANCING BEGGAR *enter.*)

OLD BEGGAR: We have come as you asked, Lord Zeami. What can we do for you?

ZEAMI: What happened? Why weren't you waiting here?

DANCING BEGGAR: We have all been in hiding. Lord Yoshitsugu said that we'd better not let anyone see us.

ZEAMI: Nonsense. That's just what I wanted you to do today—let everyone have a look at you.

DANCING BEGGAR: What do you mean?

ZEAMI: Everyone was wandering around today. You could have solicited quite a bit from them. The nobles and lords were all right here. You could have swindled them nicely. Just by telling them you were friends of Zeami.

DŌAMI: Fujiwaka! What kind of nonsense is this?

ZEAMI: Don't you think it would have been just the right sort of entertainment to accompany an imperial *nō* performance? Rumor has it that only beggars and outcasts perform here in Yoshimitsu's palace. If everyone could see that it's true, it would go a long way toward pleasing them.

DŌAMI: Is that really how you feel, Fujiwaka? Today, of all days, when the *nō* has been so honored? What pleasure can it give you to show such contempt?

ZEAMI: Contempt? That's rather an exaggeration, don't you think? Still, our art is considered in the same class with fortune telling, dancing, and all the other vulgar entertainments. We're counted among the "People of the Seven Districts."

DŌAMI: I have no idea how we are carried on the government registry books. But any child of three can tell you that *nō* rules all the arts in Japan.

ZEAMI: Yes, the *nō* may be supreme. But what of us, the actors? We can hardly be called men, let alone rulers.

DŌAMI: All you need do is to look around you. The noblemen, the courtiers, all give way before you.

ZEAMI: None have any courage. They are afraid of Yoshimitsu, who supports me . . . Yet, three days ago, I was assaulted by one voice. One voice that was not afraid. I can still hear the sound of that voice which in one breath managed to destroy me, destroy me completely. (*Softly.*) "Leave me, you outcast. Despite your rise in fortune, do not forget the circumstances of your birth." Forget them? How could I? From now on, no matter how many may throw themselves at my feet, that voice has cast me into the outer depths for all eternity. But do not mistake me. I bear no grudge. Now, everything I do is false. I may have deceived the whole country. But there remains one, at least, who is not deceived.

DŌAMI: I must have a laugh, and at your expense, Fujiwaka. You're in love with a woman and she's rejected you.

ZEAMI: No, you don't understand. That icy voice thrilled me. It filled me with happiness.

DŌAMI: But who is it? Who could have said such things to you?

ZEAMI: The name is of no importance.

HAGI: Tell me, Zeami. I want to know.

ZEAMI: And if you learn the name? What will you do?

HAGI: I will dance before her. I will show her the wretched dances of a beggar girl.

ZEAMI (*after a pause*): Very well. I will tell you. The woman is Lady Kuzuno, the daughter of Lord Michiomi, the former Minister of the Left.

DŌAMI: This is madness. Why, Lady Kuzuno is Mistress to . . .

ZEAMI: Of course. She is the favorite of my patron, Lord Yoshimitsu himself.

DŌAMI: So you want to get yourself killed then, Fujiwaka.

[29]

ZEAMI (*laughing softly*): Yes, I'm sure I do. Well then, Hagi, dance as it pleases you. As wildly, as indiscreetly as you please. And you, old woman. Frighten the nobles with your terrible prophecies. And you, old man, what about you? Why not stick your leprous nose into the sleeves of those lovely court ladies?

DŌAMI: Stop this! You are a presumptuous fool.

ZEAMI: Well, Hagi? Have you forgotten how to dance? Come, I will dance with you.

HAGI (*putting herself in position*): Lord Zeami, are you joking with me?

(*An* IMPERIAL GUARD *appears.*)

GUARD: Soon the Emperor will take his leave. All must withdraw from his presence, as is proper. (*He leaves.*)

DŌAMI: The Emperor is leaving. Fujiwaka, surely you do not wish to disturb his passage?

ZEAMI (*whispering to himself*): Lady Kuzuno. This will be the last performance of Zeami, who would serve you, and with such affection. When you hear of all this, you may be amused. For no matter how wretched the end of an outcast, it should make quite a spectacle. So then, Hagi. I wasn't lying to you. Are you prepared?

(*She nods.*)

ZEAMI: Let us dance then.

(HAGI *beats firmly on the drum tied to her waist. At that moment, the blinds of the oxcart are lifted.* LADY KUZUNO *is inside.*)

LADY KUZUNO: Since you deign to perform for me, Zeami, you really should have told me of your plans. After all, a mere actor dancing in the path of the Emperor himself, and in the garden of the palace of his own patron? What extravagant entertainment that would be! The ruler of the Shadows having an interview with the ruler of the real world. For a woman as naturally curious as I, you provide me with quite a sumptuous treat.

ZEAMI: I cannot proceed. Before you, such a performance could only be humiliating. The beauty of this moment

[30]

can only be apparent should you hear about it from others. To see me smeared with mud, tied with ropes by those ruffians. This is nothing for a lady of quality to see, I assure you.

LADY KUZUNO: But Zeami. What if I tell you that I wish to see you?

ZEAMI: Do you?

LADY KUZUNO: Yes, I do.

ZEAMI: And what is it you wish to see? Zeami's conceit? Or his wretchedness?

LADY KUZUNO: I want to see the fashion in which you risk your own death. (*Pause.*) One often speaks of a death-defying performance on the stage. But I have never witnessed such a thing. Perhaps because, as you say, such things are not considered suitable for a woman's eyes. But for once I wish to witness not a figure of speech, but the real art of facing death. And I want you, Lord Zeami, to be the one to show it to me.

ZEAMI: And so you wish me to block the path of the Emperor?

LADY KUZUNO: No, that kind of conduct will only cause difficulties for Lord Yoshimitsu. I do not require such extravagance. Here. Take this drum. It should suffice for the purpose. (*She holds out the drum to him.*)

ZEAMI: A drum?

LADY KUZUNO: I had it made especially for you. Now please strike it for me.

ZEAMI: If such is your command, I will gladly carry it out. The drum is not my special instrument, but still, I have some idea of how to use it. But, what has this drum to do with risking my life?

LADY KUZUNO: Then, you will strike the drum for me?

ZEAMI: Certainly. But why . . . ?

LADY KUZUNO: You need only to take it. The drum is the greatest masterpiece created by Ochi Kitarō.

ZEAMI (*taking the drum*): And what? What is this?

DŌAMI: What is it, Fujiwaka?

ZEAMI: The cylinder of the drum is certainly made by Ochi. But the drum is not covered with leather.

DŌAMI: What?

ZEAMI: It is not leather. It is damask.

DŌAMI: A damask drum.

ZEAMI: Lady Kuzuno. What kind of plot is this? Do you think that I can produce a sound from a damask drum?

LADY KUZUNO: So then, you do not wish to strike it? (LADY KUZUNO *motions to her* RETAINER. *He points his halberd at* ZEAMI; *as he does so, other strong* RETAINERS *surround the group.*)

DŌAMI: Fujiwaka, you have been deceived.

LADY KUZUNO (*laughing spitefully*): I find it presumptuous that a few mere theatrical performers can talk about being deceived. I thought, Zeami, that since you took an interest in me, despite the fact that you knew of my relationship with Yoshimitsu, you would know how to prepare yourself for whatever might happen. For a man to risk his life for love, without regard for his position—that is the greatest good fortune a woman can have. I want to savor this excitement to the fullest. So then. Strike the drum.

ZEAMI: And when I strike it . . . if there is no sound?

(*The* RETAINERS *push closer, pointing their halberds.*)

ZEAMI: So. You despise me for my vulgar advances because I do not know my place. You want to kill me then?

LADY KUZUNO: For a man of your artistic skill, the drum cannot fail to sound.

DŌAMI: Art is a thing of dreams; in reality, a damask drum cannot make any sound at all.

LADY KUZUNO: I certainly will not force you. If you are frightened, you may remain silent, and withdraw. There will be no punishment from me. After all your self-indulgent bragging about your despair, your own sense of shame will suffice nicely.

ZEAMI: And when I strike the drum . . . if it should sound?

LADY KUZUNO: Then it will be I, unworthy as I am, who will offer myself to you.

ZEAMI: Offer yourself . . . ?

LADY KUZUNO: In the hope that you will love me.

(*The two stare intently at each other.*)

HAGI (*with a scream*): Zeami! Do not strike the drum!

LADY KUZUNO: I see that this little dancing girl is quite concerned about you. For someone who would "set fire to the universe itself" and "dance madly alone," she seems rather weak-spirited. Is she what they call a woman of the common people? Don't worry about striking the drum then. The girl seems to suit you. Take her hand and retire.

ZEAMI: Dōami. Play your flute for me. (*With vigor.*) Play!

(DŌAMI *puts his flute to his lips.* ZEAMI *prepares himself. A terrible silence.*)

LADY KUZUNO (*her voice shaking*): Zeami. Will you strike the drum? Truly?

(*The* RETAINERS *push in another step.*)

LADY KUZUNO: You will strike it then. Zeami.

(*A piercing sound from the flute.*)

LADY KUZUNO: Lord Zeami. I understand. Now, give it up.

(ZEAMI *suddenly looks at* LADY KUZUNO. *He is tranquil.*)

HAGI: Strike, Zeami! Strike!

(*The piercing sound of the flute. As the wail rises,* ZEAMI *strikes the drum. Of course there is no sound. All cry out in dismay. The sound of the flute breaks off. After an instant, the* RETAINERS *begin to close in.*)

LADY KUZUNO (*interrupting*): It sounded. The drum sounded.

RETAINERS: There was no sound.

LADY KUZUNO: I heard the sound. I heard it.

ZEAMI: There was no sound. Do with me what you will.

(*The* RETAINERS *prepare to drag* ZEAMI *away. At this instant, a ringing voice fills the stage and with a sound so overwhelming it scarcely seems human. The voice is* YOSHIMITSU'S.)

YOSHIMITSU'S VOICE: Wait. Zeami. I wish you to strike the drum once more.

DŌAMI: Ah! The voice of Lord Yoshimitsu himself!

ZEAMI: So then, my Lord. This whole affair must be a plan of your devising.

YOSHIMITSU'S VOICE: It is not for you to pose any questions. I told you to strike the drum. Begin!

(*At the sound of the flute,* ZEAMI *takes his stance and strikes the drum. The sound echoes out clearly, issuing from somewhere in the empty sky. Everyone cries out in surprise.* ZEAMI *alone is crestfallen. He abandons his stance.*)

YOSHIMITSU'S VOICE: Good! Good, Zeami. Continue to strike the drum.

(ZEAMI *strikes the drum quickly. Rapid drumbeats fill the air. Discouraged, he stops.*)

YOSHIMITSU'S VOICE: What has happened? Why have you stopped?

ZEAMI: There is no sound. Proceed with my punishment.

YOSHIMITSU'S VOICE: Splendid! Your performance is considerably better, even, than at the imperial performance today. Lady Kuzuno belongs to you now. Take her with you.

ZEAMI: No, I must insist. The drum never sounded. It is rather death, my death you must command.

YOSHIMITSU'S VOICE: Arrogant fool! Your conceit is remarkable. Do you really think that someone like you is capable of judging whether the drum sounded or not? Everyone talks of Zeami's art. But in the end, you remain a Shadow cast by me, by Yoshimitsu's Light. Well then, all of you. Did the drum sound? Or did it not?

DŌAMI: It sounded.

RETAINERS: It sounded.

YOSHIMITSU'S VOICE: Now do you understand, Zeami? (*He laughs loudly.*)

[34]

Zeami

(*The laughing voice grows ever louder; at its greatest peak,* ZEAMI *suddenly rises and grasps the hand of* LADY KUZUNO.)

HAGI (*screaming*): There was no sound! The drum did not sound!

(*Her cries are lost in a tempest of laughter, as* ZEAMI *and* LADY KUZUNO *draw close to each other and stand together.*)

Curtain

Act Two

The same setting as Act One. The season is early spring. It is near midnight. Several sprays of wisteria can be seen in the reflected light of the watch-fires.

(SANJŌ *comes toward* ŌE, *who is standing by quietly.*)

ŌE: How is his condition then?

SANJŌ: It hardly seems possible he can last the night.

ŌE: How strange this all is. It has been less than two months since the imperial *nō* performances.

SANJŌ: Even a man like the great Yoshimitsu must meet his end. Surprising, isn't it? In the face of death, all that comes to mind are foolish commonplaces.

ŌE: Well, after all, death is something absolutely clear. Absolutely certain. There is nothing there to interpret.

[35]

SANJŌ: Yet afterwards, things remain complicated for those who are left behind. Yoshimochi and Yoshitsugu, for example. The situation will be difficult enough, whoever wins out.

ŌE: In the end, Yoshimitsu was too powerful a man. Still, Yoshitsugu does seem to have inherited something of his father's ability.

SANJŌ: Exactly. Yet take the case of the damask drum: Yoshitsugu surely wouldn't have had the strength to force a silent drum to sound.

ŌE: The damask drum? That whole affair has turned into a myth already. There's not a soul who will still maintain that it never sounded. Everyone searches their memories, and their fading recollections somehow tell them that, yes, there must have been a sound.

SANJŌ: Even Zeami, who showed so much courage then, has stopped resisting now. Because, just as you might have suspected, Lord Yoshimitsu took that insolent actor's pride and used it as a flower to further decorate his own person. I wonder, too, if a man like Yoshitsugu, even if he has talent, won't find Zeami too difficult to deal with.

ŌE: Why Lord Sanjō, I thought you certainly had a better opinion of Lord Yoshitsugu than that.

SANJŌ: Actually, I find it easier to praise a person when I have no respect for him. It's really more comfortable to say something altogether divorced from the truth.

ŌE: Oh, absolutely. In fact, that is the attitude all the nobility takes these days. This kind of thing is just what a man like Zeami doesn't seem to understand. Whether it's love or hate, he wants to bind together the man and the truth. That's why, more than anyone, he will be crushed by what's happening tonight. It's true that most seem to favor Yoshitsugu as successor to his father. But Yoshimochi may well take the power, and then Zeami must relinquish his position to his rival Zōami.

[36]

Zeami

SANJŌ. I can't help but laugh. The Light fades, and the Shadow must live on alone. Zeami now begins to seem unsteady; the last time I saw him, he looked like a kite with its strings cut, flying loose in the air. He was with a suspicious-looking old woman.

ŌE: Oh? Actually, he asked me to meet him here.

SANJŌ: At this hour? He must have urgent business.

ŌE: The other day, he told me that he had prepared something ingenious to show me. Now he suddenly sent a messenger, asking me to come. He must find his future quite uncertain. That's probably why he is in such a hurry.

SANJŌ: But here? In a place like this?

ŌE: Zeami certainly cannot leave the palace tonight. It's about time for him to arrive.

SANJŌ: What's that?

(*Shouts, the sound of crossed swords.*)

ŌE: It seems that trouble has broken out already.

SANJŌ: Lord Ōe, I wonder if this isn't that ingenious trick Zeami had ready for you? If so, I want nothing to do with it.

ŌE: I don't like this at all. Let's hide ourselves over there for a moment and watch. (*The two leave the stage.*)

(YOSHITSUGU *enters, defending himself against an attack by two* RETAINERS. ZEAMI *also enters, accompanied by the* OLD SORCERESS. *He looks with disdain on the beleaguered* YOSHITSUGU, *who finally manages to kill one of his adversaries. The other flees.*)

YOSHITSUGU: That scheme wasn't very well prepared. If Yoshimochi wants to bury me, he will have to be more ingenious than that. (*He notices* ZEAMI.) Who's there? (*On his guard.*) Who? Ah! Is it you Zeami? With that old woman beside you, you make a pair ready to welcome me to hell.

ZEAMI: That was a dangerous moment, Lord Yoshitsugu.

[37]

YOSHITSUGU: I'm not going to die. I don't want to die. No, not at all. And do you know why?

ZEAMI: Perhaps the fact that your father Lord Yoshimitsu now faces death has given you something to think about.

YOSHITSUGU: When the coffin lid goes down, the accounts are reckoned. You know that a man's value is decided once and for all, when that lid has been shut.

ZEAMI: Yes. And the value, the value of all the effort and energy of a life will be weighed in the eyes of those who surround that coffin.

YOSHITSUGU: This is just what so enrages me. To think that a great man—the one who, all through his life, was the one to put a price on everything and everybody—to think that even before that lid goes down, a price can be put on him by all those fools.

ZEAMI: Even Lord Hosokawa and Lord Akamatsu haven't been above making such judgments from time to time. They've talked about where to rank Lord Yoshimitsu among all the other Shōguns of history.

YOSHITSUGU: You know the custom, of course: since the beginning, there has always been a posthumous name assigned to an Emperor after his death. His character as a man, and all his accomplishments,. are put on the scales and weighed. They then assign some clever little name to the remains. It's said that the Emperor Shih, all the way back in the Ch'in Dynasty of China, decided to abolish the custom altogether. The rage he must have felt echoes in my own heart as well. For such a thing cannot be allowed. To lie there, exposed to the gaze of all those impertinent fools. There's no way to stare them down, if your own eyes are already closed forever.

ZEAMI: That is what death means.

YOSHITSUGU: How ironic, after all. That a man who never needed to depend on others throughout his whole life should, at the end, discover that the final accounting

must be left to others. Terrible. That is why I do not wish
to die, Zeami. I would willingly suffer many times over
the pain of death, as long as I might still remain alive. I
want to establish my own worth, myself. Can you understand me? Even if all the flesh of my body were to rot
away, I want my eyes alone to remain, so that I can go on
living.

(ZEAMI *laughs darkly.*)

YOSHITSUGU: Why do you laugh? I don't think you understand what I'm trying to say.

ZEAMI: But do you yourself understand, Lord Yoshitsugu?
There are those who, even while they are alive, must entrust the evaluation of their worth to others.

YOSHITSUGU: Are you speaking of yourself?

ZEAMI: I am only a Shadow. What can a Shadow know? What
kind of being am I? Is my true being to be found within
this something called Zeami? I cannot know even that. I
dance, but others pronounce what I do as good or bad.
You may say that in that very fact exists the real Zeami.
Or you may disagree. Yet, what else is there? In the end,
only this Shadow, reflected in the eyes of others, can
serve as my real identity.

YOSHITSUGU: If what you say is true, how simple everything
would be.

ZEAMI: Simple, did you say?

YOSHITSUGU: Don't you agree? You yourself are not encum-
bered by having to make any decisions. You are exempt
from feeling, and from desire. How can I help but envy
you? Your pride, your shame—all are determined by the
others. You remain a Shadow to their Light.

ZEAMI (*laughing darkly*): It is evident that for you, Lord Yoshitsugu, there exists no war between father and son.
Your father, Lord Yoshimitsu, has told me the same
thing many times before.

YOSHITSUGU: You know, Zeami, that after my father dies, it

[39]

will be I, Yoshitsugu, who will serve as the Light for your Shadow.

ZEAMI (*ironically*): I am grateful.

YOSHITSUGU: Light has many enemies. A Shadow too, I suppose. Did you see what just happened?

ZEAMI: Yes. All of it.

YOSHITSUGU: They were your enemies too.

ZEAMI: I understand.

YOSHITSUGU: In my brother Yoshimochi's eyes, Zeami does not exist. But you see there must be one who calls himself Zeami, who calls himself into existence.

ZEAMI: True. And every day that Zeami exists in this world, he finds humiliation anew in the eyes of Yoshimochi.

YOSHITSUGU: Come closer, Lord Zeami. If you have truly understood my words, then I have something to ask of you.

(ZEAMI, *without speaking, draws closer*.)

YOSHITSUGU: Tonight, I want you to make a trip for me.

ZEAMI: A trip? But where?

YOSHITSUGU: I've talked to you already about Lord Kitabatake, who is now in Ise. Ever since the fall of the Southern Court, he can only lament his own sad fortunes. Now I want all the more to make him my ally. (*The two exchange glances.*)

ZEAMI: And then . . . ?

YOSHITSUGU: There can be no delay. I will overthrow Yoshimochi.

ZEAMI: There will be fighting then.

YOSHITSUGU: Yes. And I will win. I have many who will fight with me—the family of Ochi in Yamato, the clan of Uesugi, in the east . . .

ZEAMI: But why is it necessary for me to serve as your messenger?

YOSHITSUGU: Because you can always find a plausible excuse for leaving the capital. Say that you are going to the

[40]

Great Shrine at Ise in order to present your offerings for the recovery of Lord Yoshimitsu. The name Zeami has more influence than many great lords might hope to possess themselves. For the people out in the country, it is as good as saying the name of Yoshimitsu himself. And, Zeami, you must persuade Kitabatake to think of his own interests. He is much dissatisfied at present. It should not be hard to convince him to take up arms against Yoshimochi. Well, then. What do you think about all this?

ZEAMI: More than twenty years ago, my father Kan'ami set out on a tour of Suruga province. His purpose, he said, was show himself, show his plays there. But my father unexpectedly died in Suruga. He was at his very peak as an artist, not even fifty years old. (*A short pause.*) For a long time, I was never able to comprehend why he went to Suruga. Now, for the first time, I feel I have understood.

YOSHITSUGU: Are you afraid to go then?

ZEAMI: Do you mean tonight?

YOSHITSUGU: Do you find the idea disagreeable?

ZEAMI (*laughing*): Lord Yoshitsugu. This evening, actually, I have planned a most stimulating entertainment for you.

YOSHITSUGU: Something interesting?

ZEAMI: Won't you consent to watch it with me? Usually I am the one who is watched by others. Tonight, I will be the one to watch, watch a performance that can only happen once in a lifetime.

YOSHITSUGU: All this is most imprudent. At a time like this. On a night as important as this one.

ZEAMI: I cannot be sure that I will even be alive tomorrow. There may be no opportunity other than tonight.

YOSHITSUGU: But I am asking you to go to Ise precisely so that you can save your life.

ZEAMI: Someone's coming.

(ŌE, SANJŌ *enter*.)

ŌE: Lord Zeami. Your summons came at a rather awkward moment. Now tell me, what is this fascinating performance you speak of?

ZEAMI: I regret having to disturb you. I realize that I should have made better preparations to receive you; I took advantage of the fact that you were already here, given the situation at the moment. Because I do have something I would particularly like to show you.

ŌE: What is it you have in mind to show us? Some new dances?

ZEAMI: Lord Ōe. I understand you posses a *nō* mask that has long been very precious to you. Do you have it with you now?

ŌE: Do you think I could ever part with it for an instant? Here it is. (*He takes out the mask.*) I would like Lord Yoshitsugu to examine the mask as well. Long ago, this mask delivered me from the power of a certain woman.

(YOSHITSUGU, *displeased, says nothing.*)

SANJŌ (*intervening*): Why yes, the two of us were speaking of that mask only this evening. We were saying that among all the warriors, only you, Lord Yoshitsugu, would appreciate the charm of the story. The mask, you see, was made in the likeness of a certain girl. And Lord Ōe went out of his way to tell her that he much preferred the mask.

ŌE: That's about the only way a man can win out over a woman. After all, it is a man's eyes that put him in love with a girl. The real battle a man has is with his own eyes. So, in desperation, what does he do? He escapes from one woman only to fall in love with another. There's no end to it, ever.

SANJŌ: As they say, a pockmark can look like a dimple. But I suppose you're right. In the end, falling in love with a woman is a function of the eyes.

[42]

ŌE: Exactly. Know that fact and you are the victor. But your
eyes must earn their victory for themselves. After all,
when you compare a real woman with her image, it's not
easy to transfer your passion to a Shadow. Animal passion is a hindrance. Compassion is an enemy as well. But
if a man can overcome all that and be completely captivated by the image he himself has created, then he can
free himself from women forever.

SANJŌ: Come now, Lord Ōe, I don't find your conduct quite
as uncontaminated as all that. I remember an incident at
Mibu, with a dancing girl . . .

ŌE: Desire is a fact. But since that time, my deepest emotions
have never been involved. No woman has ever won out
over this mask.

ZEAMI: Then it is the woman who should be pitied, Lord
Yoshitsugu. As far as I'm concerned, this is nothing but a
piece of carved wood.

SANJŌ: I'm not surprised. You are not a man who sees. You
are a Shadow. A subtle, exquisite apparition created in
the eyes of Lord Yoshimitsu.

ŌE: Exactly so. With Lord Yoshimitsu, it is not merely a
question of women. He has always been determined to
win out over all the beautiful things in the world. He has
allowed nothing to seduce him—not the bravery of the
warriors, not the wisdom of the elders, not the awe-
someness of the Emperor himself. He has always wished
to transcend, to defeat everything he has found beautiful
in creation. And indeed, Lord Zeami, this is how you
came to be created. A likeness capable of reflecting all the
myriad wonders of the world. A living counterfeit. Has
that not truly been your role?

ZEAMI: It seems, Lord Ōe, you really understand Lord Yoshimitsu's most intimate thoughts.

ŌE: Loving a woman brings torments enough. How excruci-
ating then, for a man to love a whole country. (*Holding up*

[43]

the mask.) Surely that is why he created an imitation of the world. He wanted to forget the real one from time to time.

ZEAMI: Do you think the real world can be forgotten? (*A low laugh*.) Reality will pursue you, wherever you are. One day, that mask will suddenly show itself to you as a piece of wood, painted in fading colors.

ŌE: Perhaps, to eyes that lack sufficient strength. Only the strength of a nobleman can give life to the image of a phantom.

ZEAMI (*with a certain austerity*): Then, Lord Ōe, I beg to show you something that will test the powers of discernment of those eyes. Old woman, come here!

(*The* OLD SORCERESS *comes forward and takes a fan from her robes.* ŌE *takes the fan from her and looks at it with some suspicion.*)

ŌE: What . . . what is this?

ZEAMI: I'm sure you have a fan just like this one. Kindly compare them.

(ŌE *takes out his own and examines them both.*)

ŌE: They are the same. Exactly the same. How . . . how did she get hold of this?

ZEAMI: That is not the question. Look rather at the face of this woman who owns the fan. Look carefully.

(ŌE *and the* OLD SORCERESS *look at each other.*)

ŌE (*screaming*): A lie! A lie! It's a lie!

ZEAMI: How can there be any question of an imposter? The woman was known only to you . . . thirty years ago. Lord Ōe. There is no mistake. She is . . . (*A low laugh.*)

(ŌE *reels backwards.*)

OLD SORCERESS (*laughing*): Of course. You see now what has become of that girl you cast aside. From this night on, my Lord, the past, in the person of this living form before you, will never leave your side.

ŌE: This is some kind of terrible plot. Lord Yoshitsugu, you must help me. Or wait—did you have a hand in all this too?

(YOSHITSUGU *suddenly breaks out in cruel laughter.*)

ZEAMI: A moving encounter, don't you think? Surely you must agree that I have provided you with some interesting entertainment: the reunion of two who exchanged fans and traded vows. Thirty years ago.

ŌE: Hideous. Change has made her a travesty of what she was when I knew her. More hideous yet, there remains in this crumbling countenance something of what it was before. Zeami, you have played a cruel trick on me. My dream of thirty years is shattered.

ZEAMI: Why should that be? The face of an old woman or two—how could they triumph over that face on your mask?

(ŌE *examines the mask.*)

ŌE: It's no use. The mask has lost its power. This mask, which could rival the beauty of any radiant face, now seems hollow and lifeless. While her face, as weathered as that of an old Buddha, now seems to possess all the vigor of a real woman. My wooden mask, always so beautiful, seems dreary and without any life of its own now.

ZEAMI: Gather your strength, Lord Ōe. With your powers of discernment, you can surely determine whether or not there may be any truth in Shadows.

ŌE: I can see nothing. The mask. The mask must help me. (*Speaking to the mask.*) Lend me your strength! Your strength!

ZEAMI (*suppressing a laugh*): What can you expect a Shadow to accomplish? From now on, this old woman will never leave your side. She will always remain before your eyes. And you, Lord Ōe, can test your eyes as much as you will.

ŌE: Betrayed. I've been betrayed by a Shadow.

(ŌE, *helped by* SANJŌ, *leaves the stage.* ZEAMI, *watching them, laughs softly, then more loudly.*)

YOSHITSUGU: Why, Zeami? Why have you let me see all this?

ZEAMI: There's no particular reason. Or perhaps I merely thought to show you that, after all, a Shadow cannot have strength enough to help the Light.

YOSHITSUGU: Do you mean . . . that you plan to betray me too?

ZEAMI: How can a Shadow without substance make any such plot? A Shadow must remain, as always, a Shadow. And nothing but a Shadow.

OLD SORCERESS: Lord Zeami, do you really intend to say no more than that?

YOSHITSUGU: Old woman, what is Zeami really scheming for?

OLD SORCERESS (*shaking her head*): I do not know. But whatever follows will surely be more horrible for Lord Zeami than for anyone else.

YOSHITSUGU: I am completely confused. But at least I think I understand that you, Zeami, do not want to go to Ise. Is that so?

(ZEAMI *remains silent, distracted.*)

YOSHITSUGU: Well, then. Stay here. (*He swirls around and leaves the stage.*)

ZEAMI: What did you mean, old lady? When you asked me if I had said everything I had intended to say?

OLD SORCERESS: I meant when you said: "A Shadow must remain, as always, a Shadow. And nothing but a Shadow."

ZEAMI: But do you understand? Do you understand what I am trying to accomplish? I don't yet know what it is that I've set out to do.

OLD SORCERESS: Eyes that merely make a pretense of Light soon cloud over. But Lord Yoshimitsu's Light will not be darkened so easily.

ZEAMI: That is true. That much I understand. At the very

[46]

moment we were amusing ourselves over Lord Ōe, I felt the strength of Lord Yoshimitsu's eyes. And his tenacity.

OLD SORCERESS: If you have understood this much, then the events that follow will explain themselves to you. But there is one thing you must remember. Before you die yourself, you will kill many others. Even those who are close to you. To begin with, Hagi is already dead. The very night of the damask drum.

ZEAMI: True. And she had a daughter, I understand.

OLD SORCERESS: Her name is Kikyō. She is five years old now.

ZEAMI: If there is no one else to help her, I will keep her with me.

OLD SORCERESS: That would be a good thing. But would that really bring the girl any happiness?

(ZEAMI *looks with gentleness on the* OLD SORCERESS.)

(LADY KUZUNO *enters, in a state of great agitation.*)

LADY KUZUNO: Lord Zeami! What are you doing here, of all places? I've looked everywhere for you. Everywhere.

ZEAMI: Tonight, Lord Yoshimitsu faces his most critical hour. You must not leave his bedside, even for a moment.

LADY KUZUNO: But Yoshimochi and his retainers are jostling about there; I cannot approach Yoshimitsu. Yoshimochi wants to bend Lord Yoshimitsu's last testament around to serve his own ends. Lord Zeami, in one night Yoshimochi has thrown off his disguise. He is no longer a cautious rat; now he is a wolf. And he shows his fangs.

ZEAMI: That was to be expected.

LADY KUZUNO: You and I have been the ones most favored by Lord Yoshimitsu. We cannot permit such viciousness.

ZEAMI: Viciousness?

LADY KUZUNO: What could be more vicious than trying to twist the dying words of one's own father? And in the end, whatever Yochimochi does will only cause more danger to you and to Lord Yoshitsugu.

[47]

(*At this,* LORD YOSHITSUGU *enters silently.*)

ZEAMI: I appreciate your concern. But my own life is worthless. Better go and tell Lord Yoshitsugu of your worries
yourself. (ZEAMI *begins to take his leave.*)

LADY KUZUNO: Then Lord Zeami. You have no concern for
me?

ZEAMI: What?

LADY KUZUNO: You are the only one I can confide in, you are
the only one who can help.

ZEAMI: And why me?

LADY KUZUNO (*a silence; then with gravity*): Less than two
months have passed. Since that night.

ZEAMI: I am filled with chagrin. That was the sport of a passing moment. I had forgotten all about it.

LADY KUZUNO: Then listen to this. Lord Yoshimochi has said
that he will take me by force.

(ZEAMI *turns and looks at her sharply.*)

LADY KUZUNO: I see I moved your heart a little then. I am
telling you the truth. I belong to the Shōgun, he said,
and Yoshimochi intends to keep me, by force if necessary.

(ZEAMI *stares at her, without saying a word.*)

YOSHITSUGU (*coming forward*): But why you? You, who more
than any other, were first in my father's affection?

LADY KUZUNO: That is exactly the reason. Don't think he desires me, or feels any tenderness for me. He wants to
possess everything that his father Lord Yoshimitsu possessed. That is the only reason.

YOSHITSUGU: But my father is still alive.

LADY KUZUNO (*to* ZEAMI): Yoshimochi said all this right beside Yoshimitsu's pillow. He said he would take everything his father possessed, even if he destroys himself in
the process. That is, except Zeami . . .

YOSHITSUGU: Except Zeami? What does that mean?

[48]

LADY KUZUNO: Zeami, he said, was too soiled from his father's hands. He should be buried, along with Lord Yoshimitsu's other personal effects.

YOSHITSUGU: Zeami? Did you hear that?

(ZEAMI *remains silent but does not turn away.*)

YOSHITSUGU: Think again, Lady Kuzuno. Does my brother know that you and Zeami have been on intimate terms? Even if only once?

LADY KUZUNO (*to* ZEAMI): I told him that as well, hoping it would serve as some kind of pretext for him to reject me. But Yoshimochi only laughed. Zeami's not really a man at all, he said. Whatever he seems to be in body, in his heart he is less than a man, even less than a eunuch of China. There is nothing there, he told me, you've been made love to by a Shadow.

YOSHITSUGU (*as if in pursuit*): Zeami!

ZEAMI (*after a pause*): What is it that you want me to do?

LADY KUZUNO: Take me with you. Anywhere. To Yamato. To Yoshino. I'll tell fortunes, I'll become a dancer, anything. Anything, rather than become mistress to Lord Yoshimochi.

ZEAMI (*shaking his head*): No. You have no idea of what is involved. I'll not even mention the hunger, the cold. But do you know what it is really like to be treated with contempt?

LADY KUZUNO: Better to receive the scorn of simpletons than the embraces of a nobleman I despise.

ZEAMI: Yet you . . . you, who have entrusted your body to me . . .

LADY KUZUNO: Lord Zeami, you are too cruel. Must I say everything? (*A pause.*) I have told you already . . . that I love you.

ZEAMI: What?

LADY KUZUNO: I first told you so a long, long time ago.

ZEAMI (*after a pause; with great seriousness*): I risked my life. And for your sake.

LADY KUZUNO: Yes. And I decided then that if something happened to you, I would give up my life as well.

ZEAMI: I cannot believe you.

LADY KUZUNO: I have kept still the farewell note I prepared. I wrote that I was deeply grieved over the whole heartless jest, and that Yoshimitsu would now lose both his favorite amusements—you, and me—all at once.

ZEAMI (*sharply*): And I suppose when you told him this, Lord Yoshimochi just laughed. Laughed, and said that it was nothing. That you had been tricked by a Shadow.

LADY KUZUNO: Yoshimochi said that if Akamatsu or Hosokawa had done such a thing, no clemency could be permitted. But if it was only Zeami, he said . . . and then he laughed. Even his father, Lord Yoshimitsu himself, he told me . . .

ZEAMI (*sharply*): What do you mean? That Lord Yoshimitsu himself . . .

LADY KUZUNO: . . . his father, too, just laughed and forgave you, that time.

ZEAMI: I'm sure that is exactly what Lord Yoshimochi said.

LADY KUZUNO (*uneasily*): What do you mean?

ZEAMI (*a pause; he paces slowly; then, with great seriousness*): Never mind. For a long time I've been sure that is just how it must have been. Do you remember? Lord Yoshimitsu's voice then, when he laughed. Now I understand everything quite clearly. The reason why, on that day, he pardoned me.

YOSHITSUGU: Are you dissatisfied that he spared your life?

ZEAMI (*laughing*): What dissatisfaction could I possibly feel? A Shadow is not permitted any such luxuries.

YOSHITSUGU: If that is so, then go. Go to Kitabatake at Ise. Yoshimochi's hand is already at your throat.

[50]

LADY KUZUNO: Wherever you go, you must take me with you. Lord Zeami, I beg you to give me shelter.

YOSHITSUGU: What is it, Zeami? Why do you hesitate?

(ZEAMI *is silent. He shakes his head.*)

YOSHITSUGU: You cannot say that you are powerless. There are people all over this country who hold you in high regard. And when the moment arrives, every outcast in every province will join together to help you.

LADY KUZUNO: And you, who were so close to Lord Yoshimitsu. If you let it be known that your master made some kind of secret testament, there are many warriors who will hurry to support you, Lord Yoshitsugu.

YOSHITSUGU: Of course. And that is just what my father would have wanted. If you let Yoshimochi take the power, it is my father you are betraying.

ZEAMI (*sharply*): I decline.

YOSHITSUGU: Have you no sense of gratitude? Illness has destroyed my father's body. But do you want it said that Zeami has extinguished his Light?

LADY KUZUNO: Have you no pity? Even after a woman like myself has thrown herself on your mercy?

ZEAMI (*after a pause*): But Lord Yoshitsugu, you just saw, didn't you? Lord Ōe, with his mask of a woman? You know, then, that a Shadow has not the strength to assist the Light.

YOSHITSUGU: You are no mask carved of wood. You are a man, with blood coursing through your veins. You must be.

ZEAMI (*sharply*): And when did that happy transformation come about?

YOSHITSUGU (*a pause*): What are you trying to say?

ZEAMI: Only a moment ago, you told me that you envied me. Because I was a Shadow, freed from all the realities of living men. And your father, Lord Yoshimitsu, said precisely the same thing. "Zeami is such a lucky fellow. He has no need to think, no need to feel."

YOSHITSUGU: But even a Shadow has to know his Light. Has to know his Master. Choose then. Will it be Yoshitsugu? Or Yoshimochi?

ZEAMI: But haven't you already explained the whole thing yourself? I've not had any choices to make in forty years. My decision? How ridiculous. I can be no more helpful than a paper lantern hung out in the blinding light of noon.

YOSHITSUGU: Very well, amuse yourself. But the time for a choice has come. Even for those like you.

ZEAMI (*laughing in a low voice*): Is that so? Has the time finally come? (*Sharply.*) Well, Zeami declines to make a choice.

LADY KUZUNO: Zeami, in a woman's eyes there exists neither Light nor Shadow. All I see is a man I know I can trust. And, Zeami, I ask now for your help.

YOSHITSUGU: I know what is needed. Zeami. Today you can consider yourself reborn. As a warrior. The world will know you now as, say, Hatanosaemon. How do you like that? Isn't that a proper-sounding name?

ZEAMI: I see. A man can be made an outcast, and an outcast made a man, all by the force of Lord Yoshitsugu's will. Well I, a Shadow, with no force and no will, have still one thing that I can do.

YOSHITSUGU: Then tell me what it is.

ZEAMI: I, by my own choice, can decide to remain a Shadow.

OLD SORCERESS: Lord Zeami . . .

ZEAMI: I was born and raised to be a Shadow. Until tonight. And from tonight . . .

(*Voices can suddenly be heard: sounds of wailing from within* YOSHIMITSU's *palace. A* RETAINER *appears.*)

RETAINER: Lord Yoshimitsu is no more. He has hidden himself from us forever.

ZEAMI: From tonight on, I shall remain the Shadow that I have chosen to be.

(YOSHITSUGU *and* LADY KUZUNO *stare at* ZEAMI *for a moment without moving; then they manage to stumble offstage. The* OLD SORCERESS *comes forward.*)

OLD SORCERESS: So you have finally spoken, Lord Zeami. But do you really understand the frightening decision you have made? For the end of all this will be terrible.

ZEAMI: I think I do understand. It may be the arrogance of an instant. For the Shadow, too, seems all the starker in that one final instant as the Light fades. Soon, it fades as well. (*Forcefully.*) But let no one say I was denied that instant.

Curtain

Act Three

Ten years have passed since Act Two. ZEAMI *is now in his mid-fifties.*

ZEAMI's *house. The forestage represents a garden; behind, a house, surrounded by a veranda. The decor, again, should not be realistic. The checkered dividing wall from Act One can serve now to suggest a wall and the raised shutters of the veranda. To the side stands an object with a curious shape, suggesting some sort of statue, wrapped in white cloth. Steps lead from the veranda to the garden. Garden shrubs at stage left. Snow has fallen. The stage in Act Two remained dark. This act is blindingly bright.*

[53]

(*As the curtain rises, the* OLD BEGGAR *and the* DANCING BEGGAR, *both now older in appearance, are teaching a song to* KIKYŌ. *She is now about fifteen or sixteen. She bears a certain resemblance to* HAGI.)

DANCING BEGGAR: That's right. That's it. Stamp your foot firmly. Good. Now, sing the song again.

KIKYO: But before long, Lord Zeami . . .

OLD BEGGAR: Don't worry about that. He will be all the more delighted to know that you have learned it. So try the song again.

DANCING BEGGAR: Yes. Try.

KIKYŌ (*singing*):
"I'm glad the nightingale is dead.
I'm glad the flowers fall.
Set fire to the universe itself!
I will dance on, madly dance, alone! . . ."

(ZEAMI *enters. He is extremely cross.*)

ZEAMI: Kikyō! What do you think you're doing?

KIKYŌ: I'm singing . . . my mother's song.

ZEAMI: Your mother's song? And who taught it to you?

KIKYŌ: These two old men here.

ZEAMI: So that's what you've been up to. And did you bring what I asked you to?

DANCING BEGGAR: We certainly wouldn't fail you, would we? It's over there.

ZEAMI: I see. Bring it here then. And take off the wrappings.

(*The two bring the statue and unwrap it. The sculpture is revealed as a statue of the Buddha, about three feet high, carved by the great master Kaikei.**)

KIKYŌ: Oh! What a beautiful statue. Why is it here?

* fl. c. 1185–1220.

[54]

Zeami

DANCING BEGGAR: Because we stole it. From the Jōkaku temple, in the Sixth Ward. Just the two of us.

KIKYŌ: From the Jōkaku temple? A holy statue of the Buddha? What do you intend to do with it?

ZEAMI: Kikyō. Don't listen to those two.

OLD BEGGAR: What? What do you mean?

ZEAMI: Here is the money I promised you. You've been paid. Now go home at once.

DANCING BEGGAR: Zeami, wait now . . .

ZEAMI: You have no reason to question what I say. And from now on, keep away from Kikyō. I've adopted her. She is now officially a daughter in my family. The Kanze family.

DANCING BEGGAR: Well what do you think of that? Her poor mother Hagi was nothing more than a street dancer. I wonder what she would say.

ZEAMI: What would she say? Don't teach her daughter such a song—that's what she would say.

DANCING BEGGAR: But would Hagi have wanted her daughter to become so superior? And forget all the songs of the street dancers?

ZEAMI: You don't understand anything. Neither Hagi's song nor her feelings when she sang that song.

OLD BEGGAR: Let's go. Lord Zeami is no longer the man he once was. When he had Lord Yoshimitsu as his patron, he didn't mind being seen with beggars and outcasts. But with a new Shōgun, we've become just an embarrassment to him.

DANCING BEGGAR: Lord Zeami, you must understand the situation as well as anyone else. Lord Yoshitsugu, who gave you his support, was defeated in battle. No one even knows where to find him now. Think what dangers there are in your future. You surely don't think you can get along without us.

ZEAMI: I see you are still here.

OLD BEGGAR (*with a sigh*): Now is the time you need us most. And yet you want to struggle on alone. I suppose men like us can no longer comprehend what goes on inside the head of the great Lord Zeami.

DANCING BEGGAR: Let's leave then. But just a word of warning, Zeami. You are head of the Kanze family now. And proud of it. But remember. That family is a flowering branch that sprang from the trunk of our own tree. If you cut the trunk, the blossoms lose all their reason to flower. (*The two leave the stage.*)

(ZEAMI *approaches the statue.*)

ZEAMI: Those men . . . such men appear to be real outcasts, real performers . . . yet, in their hearts . . . (*He looks carefully at the Buddha's face.*) Yes. Truly a great work of art. Kaikei made it two hundred years ago. And it is a masterpiece.

KIKYŌ (*singing to herself*):
"I'm glad the nightingale is dead,
I'm glad the flowers fall . . ."

ZEAMI (*with tenderness*): Kikyō. Please don't sing that song.

KIKYŌ: Don't you like it? You don't like the song?

ZEAMI: Your mother sang that song in the gardens of the great Shōgun Yoshimitsu. And she died the same night. That song poured forth from the depths of her heart. Then she began to vomit blood, and soon after she died.

KIKYŌ: Did you take care of her?

ZEAMI: What?

KIKYŌ: I am old enough to understand. I'm already sixteen.

ZEAMI (*after a pause*): Well, then. No, that night, I was taken up with quite another woman.

KIKYŌ: Then the song is an unlucky one. At least for a woman. But I must go on singing it. For my mother's sake. For the sake of the agony she suffered.

ZEAMI: Nonsense. That song has nothing to do with a woman's suffering.

[56]

KIKYŌ: Whose suffering then? That of an outcast doomed to wander?

ZEAMI: Do you really think you can understand the meaning of that song? In your heart?

KIKYŌ: No, I don't. But I like the song very much.

ZEAMI: A performer sings that song when he is ready to die. And when the song is finished, death is the only thing that remains. Across the burnt-out ashes that stretch on as far as the eye can reach, you dance on, all alone, no one to hear you, no one to see you . . . You dance madly on. Everyone of us has felt this in his heart as he performs for the applause of others all his life long.

KIKYŌ: The song seems terrifying now. And yet those old men seemed to enjoy teaching it to me.

ZEAMI: Men like that are always ready to make any emotion into the subject of some vile comic entertainment. A song like that conjures up blood spurting from the very heart. Yet they twist it around into some banal, catchy little song. I suppose they think that their profession entitles them to do it. There are many like that, even among the performers of *nō*.

KIKYŌ: Soon there will be a contest of *nō* plays at the Daigo temple. That's what I heard.

ZEAMI: Yes.

KIKYŌ: I am sorry for you, Zeami. Now that you have lost your backing, it must be very painful for you to have to compete, just like all the others.

ZEAMI: Who told you this?

KIKYŌ: No one told me anything. I see your two sons, Lord Motomasa and Lord Motoyoshi; they rehearse from dawn to midnight. They don't even notice me anymore.

ZEAMI: Why Kikyō! Are you in love with either of my sons?

KIKYŌ: Certainly not! (*She sings.*)
Young, they take themselves for wise,
And no one comes to woo them;

[57]

Old, alone, they feel chagrin:
Shall I tell you how I feel?

ZEAMI: You are singing about things beyond your age. But tell me, Kikyō, do you dislike me so?

KIKYŌ: I've been thinking. To tell you the truth, I wonder if you are not my real father.

ZEAMI: What are you saying?

KIKYŌ: If not, then why do I have this helpless feeling? And I understand less and less of the things you tell me. I feel as though I were going to end up in some far, far place. That's how you make me feel.

ZEAMI: Are you . . . afraid of me then?

KIKYŌ: Yes. These days you are completely absorbed. You seem like a ghost to me. Or a Shadow.

ZEAMI (*with a vigorous laugh*): Like a Shadow? I haven't heard that word for ten years now.

(MOTOYOSHI *rushes in, followed by* ZEAMI's *wife,* TSUBAKI, *who stands quietly to the rear.*).

MOTOYOSHI: Father, Father, what's all this?

ZEAMI: What are you so upset about, Motoyoshi?

MOTOHOSHI: But Father! This Buddha!

ZEAMI: Yes, the sacred mage of the Jōkaku Temple.

MOTOYOSHI: But what do you mean by having it stolen?

ZEAMI (*laughing lightly*): The face is extraordinary. Carvers no longer possess such skills as those. The face will make a superb mask. And with it, we will surely win the contest at the Daigo temple.

MOTOYOSHI: That face? You mean . . .

ZEAMI: Of course. I'm going to cut it off and use it for a mask.

MOTOYOSHI: How absurd! What kind of divine punishment will you call down on yourself?

ZEAMI: Motoyoshi. Take your sword. I want you to cut off the head of this Buddha.

MOTOYOSHI: Never, Father. I would rather die.

[58]

ZEAMI: Die? Why not say that you would rather go to hell? That you would wander in the most dreadful abysses? But that you had to win that contest of *nō?*

MOTOYOSHI: Father, such talk is not worthy of you. You yourself say that any such victory must come from an absolute devotion to the art of *nō* itself.

ZEAMI: You are too lenient with yourself, Motoyoshi. This devotion you speak of is no petty skill. That devotion to snatch victory from defeat must always have something, as you put it, unworthy about it.

MOTOYOSHI: There is still this to be said: the eyes of the spectators will determine the victory. But in the totality of human life, the real and final judgement will rest in the eyes of the Buddha. Can you not tell which of these two tests is the more important?

ZEAMI (*in a rather forlorn voice*): Don't speak to me like that. Don't you think I fear the wrath of the eyes of Buddha? A *nō* performer must meditate on all this while he goes on, on to entrust everything to the eyes of those who watch him. (*With a shout.*) I said cut. So cut, Motoyoshi!

MOTOYOSHI: I cannot.

ZEAMI: Motomasa! Bring your sword here! Motomasa!

(MOTOMASA *enters.*)

MOTOMASA: Did you call me, Father?

ZEAMI: I did. Remember, you are heir to the family and to its traditions. I want you to cut off the head of this Buddha.

MOTOMASA: What?

ZEAMI: It will serve as a mask in the *nō* contest. Don't mark up the face. Now cut!

MOTOMASA (*after a long pause*): Yes, Father. (*He takes out his sword.*)

MOTOYOSHI: Mother! Mother! Can't you say something to make Father stop? The wrath of the Buddha will descend on him. Please. Please stop him.

(TSUBAKI *says nothing. She remains absolutely still.*)

[59]

MOTOYOSHI: Father, you must understand. Our family is in greater and greater danger. First because of the death of Lord Yoshimitsu, long ago, and now because of the defeat of Lord Yoshitsugu. Mother wishes only for the peace and tranquillity of our house. She has been making prayers before this very Buddha for our safety. The term of her vow is finished today. Knowing all this, Father, do you still want to destroy the statue?

ZEAMI: Do you hear him, Motomasa?

MOTOMASA: Yes.

ZEAMI (*softly*): Cut.

(MOTOMASA *strikes the statue three times, cutting off the head.* KIKYŌ *and* MOTOYOSHI *turn away in horror.* TSUBAKI *remains, ever still, without flinching.*)

ZEAMI (*tenderly*): Was it painful for you, Motoyoshi? Those who watch our art demand this of us. You may well detest the audience that watches you. A great performance may require that.

MOTOYOSHI: In your performances there lingers always the odor of death. My grandfather Kan'ami said that the *nō* should earn the affection, and the respect, of all. That is the kind of actor I wish to become. (*With this, he leaves the stage.*)

ZEAMI (*to himself*): Yes, the performance should earn the respect and the esteem of all. The art. But not the actor.

(MOTOMASA, *holding the head of the Buddha in front of him, prepares to leave.*)

ZEAMI: Wait. Motomasa. Let me see that sword. (*He examines it.*)

ZEAMI: There's no mistake. That is Lord Yoshitsugu's sword. Motomasa. Where did you get this?

MOTOMASA: Lord Yoshitsugu has returned. Last month, after his plot was discovered, he managed to escape the capital. But the Shōgun has made intensive inquiries about him everywhere; he has nowhere to go. He is very much a changed man now.

ZEAMI: But Motomasa . . . you and Lord Yoshitsugu? Only a fool would shelter him now.

MOTOMASA: Lord Yoshitsugu was a patron of our family. And I am heir to that family.

ZEAMI: I would like to meet him. Bring him to me.

(TSUBAKI *leaves.* YOSHITSUGU *enters.*)

YOSHITSUGU: There's no need to call me. There's nowhere else for me to go.

ZEAMI: Lord Yoshitsugu. It seems such a long time since we last met.

YOSHITSUGU: Zeami. I am a man without honor. For I could not bear to end my own life.

ZEAMI: Yes . . . yes, I remember now. On that night when Lord Yoshimitsu died, you told me that you never wanted to die . . .

YOSHITSUGU: Ten years ago. I have gone on living, all those ten years. Yet I am still afraid. I still do not possess the courage to entrust my value to the eyes of others. And as the dust and grime of the years pile up, I become more and more afraid of the eyes of the others. But you, Zeami. You seem no older. What mysterious strength manages to keep you always so young?

ZEAMI: Shadows do not grow old.

YOSHITSUGU: And what a splendid face you have. Your expression seems solid, secure, forged over the years by all the eyes that have looked on you. In that expression, I can read no emotions whatever. Yet behind that face, what are you really thinking?

ZEAMI: Lord Yoshitsugu. What is it that you hope for, here?

YOSHITSUGU: There is not much that I can hope for. Only that, with your strength, you might hide me. I know, I know how you must feel. Nevertheless, I ask this of you.

[61]

At the least, help me to join that band of wandering entertainers. You know, the ones who were here once.

ZEAMI: Most of them are dead already. It's a cheerless life they lead. Yet even when such performers die, the race does not vanish altogether. Kikyō, come here.

YOSHITSUGU: Yes! I remember. That's the girl who . . .

ZEAMI: She is Hagi's daughter. You see, they go on forever. They never grow old.

YOSHITSUGU: Yes, Zeami, I understand. It is only we who know such agonies. You have won.

ZEAMI: Kikyō. Please show Lord Yoshitsugu to the guest quarters in back.

MOTOMASA: So you accept then, Father? You will support Lord Yoshitsugu?

ZEAMI: Support him?

MOTOMASA: Yes, Father. We must contact Lord Kitabatake in Ise and the Ochi family in Yoshino. We must rally support for Lord Yoshitsugu.

ZEAMI: You have already discussed this with Lord Yoshitsugu, I see. Useless nonsense. Use your spare time to rehearse for the *nō* performances.

MOTOMASA: No Father. These contest performances of *nō* are nothing more than a vile trick of the Shōgun, a pretext to make us look ridiculous. No matter how well we perform, we know we will lose. We can never win. We must overthrow Yoshimochi.

ZEAMI: Fool! And your brother is no better. Neither of you understands anything.

MOTOMASA: I can't comprehend you. Lately, I really don't understand you at all. You will not follow Lord Yoshimochi. And you will not help Lord Yoshitsugu. You attach yourself to no one. Father, who do you think your enemies really are?

ZEAMI: I am between Light and Darkness. The Shadow has no path to follow.

MOTOMASA: This is all beyond me. As for me, I would seek out the Darkness.

ZEAMI: The choice is not that easily made.

(TSUBAKI *enters.*)

TSUBAKI: There is a visitor here to see you, Zeami.

ZEAMI: Coming unannounced? Who is it?

TSUBAKI: It is Lady Kuzuno. She has come secretly, alone.

(*Each character, with his own memories, registers surprise.* MOTO-MASA *looks at his father, then stares at his mother. Her expression does not change; she endures everything.* MOTOMASA *cannot bear this; he leaves.*)

YOSHITSUGU: Lady Kuzuno? She is now the favorite of my brother Yoshimochi, on a rank with his own wife. Zeami, does she come here often? (ZEAMI *shakes his head no.*) (*To* TSUBAKI): Did you say that she came alone, unattended? (TSUBAKI *nods.*) Is this her first visit? (TSUBAKI *nods again.*) Zeami, surely you won't refuse. You will meet her, won't you? Why are you silent? See her. I want to see her. (*To* TSUBAKI.) I will see her.

(LADY KUZUNO *enters.* YOSHITSUGU, *delighted, begins to move toward her, but* ZEAMI *coldly restrains him and hurriedly confronts her.*)

LADY KUZUNO: At last, at long last, I found a pretext to come to you. This once . . . and after ten years. Have I changed a great deal, Zeami?

ZEAMI: A pretext, you said.

LADY KUZUNO (*laughing*): Not because of what the others might think. I fear no one now, not even the Shōgun, Yoshimochi himself. The pretext, Zeami, has to do with you. It is you I have been afraid of.

ZEAMI: And today?

LADY KUZUNO: Zeami. You are surrounded.

YOSHITSUGU: Do they know? That I am here?

LADY KUZUNO (*nodding*): Orders were given to arrest not only Lord Yoshitsugu but your whole family as well. Your

[63]

house is completely sealed off. There is no possibility of escape.

(MOTOMASA *rushes in, in great agitation.*)

MOTOMASA: Father! There's a crowd of warriors at the back gate. And mounted soldiers in front! (*He rushes away.*)

LADY KUZUNO: Now you know the reason I came. Finally, the time has come for me to give some strength to you. I've waited for this day. And for a long time. I feel as though I should thank you.

ZEAMI: Did you come to explain the danger . . . for my sake?

LADY KUZUNO: No. For mine.

ZEAMI (*after a pause*): Tsubaki. Take Kikyō and escape as best you can. (*The two leave.*)

ZEAMI: Tell me what you have to say.

LADY KUZUNO: I will come straight to the point. I am at an age when I no longer feel shame . . . I want you.

YOSHITSUGU: How attractive! And how truly gallant! A person of base breeding could never speak out like that.

ZEAMI: Would you dare to speak those words before Lord Yoshimochi?

LADY KUZUNO: Lord Yoshimochi has a quick temper, it's true, but he is a very weak man. I don't believe he would have the courage to kill a woman just because she became infatuated with an actor.

YOSHITSUGU: I am astonished. How ten years can bring about so many changes in a person.

LADY KUZUNO: Especially to a woman. And yet, in another way, women never change at all. I am reduced to the status of mistress to a man I detest. Yet I am the same woman you knew so long ago.

ZEAMI: True indeed. As time passes, you become more than ever the Lady Kuzuno I knew before.

LADY KUZUNO: If so, then why do you always avoid me? I have written to you. Sent messengers to you. And how many times have I brought my carriage before your very

[64]

gates? (ZEAMI *nods*.) Then what is it? Zeami, do you mean to persecute me? I am without a protector, without help. My fate is not of my own choosing.

ZEAMI: I have nothing to say against Lord Yoshimochi.

LADY KUZUNO: No, no, you must. You do. Help me, Lord Yoshitsugu. You are a man of rank. Help me, if you feel any pity for me.

ZEAMI (*with humor*): How curious is love. The weak are given strength. And those who would remain strong are weakened.

YOSHITSUGU: Then, Zeami, let her plea come from me as well. Listen with good grace to her real feelings.

ZEAMI: I see. Will you then ask for help from me as well?

YOSHITSUGU: And what is wrong with that? A heart healed, a life saved.

LADY KUZUNO: Lord Zeami, do not consider me as utterly defiled. I love you so desperately. That is why I resort to threats, and to blandishments. I am like a wounded deer, driven, cornered in a last extremity. Understand me.

(ZEAMI *claps his hands.* KIKYŌ *appears. He whispers something to her.* KIKYŌ *nods and leaves.* ZEAMI *stares at* LADY KUZUNO. *A pause.*)

ZEAMI: Lady Kuzuno. I have not seen you for ten years. And the reason is that I am in love with you.

LADY KUZUNO: What? What is this you tell me?

ZEAMI: What malice could I possibly bear you? If I saw you, I knew my resolve would collapse and that I would be lost. I was afraid of that. Here is the proof. I have never touched my wife all these years. Let this stand as a mark of my fidelity.

LADY KUZUNO: If you have always felt so tenderly toward me, then why not manifest that love now? Do men really lack the courage to show their love, do they feel foolish in revealing themselves?

(KIKYŌ *returns. She carries a drum.*)

ZEAMI: It is not a question of cowardice. Nor of moral scruple.

LADY KUZUNO: Then . . .

YOSHITSUGU: Then why, Zeami . . . ?

ZEAMI: Here. This is the reason for everything.

LADY KUZUNO: Oh! The drum! That drum!

YOSHITSUGU: The damask drum?

(ZEAMI *takes his stance as if to strike the drum.*)

LADY KUZUNO: You are tenacious, Zeami. You want to force me to recall everything.

ZEAMI: What I want to know does not pertain to the past. What I want to know concerns both of us. Now. Today. (ZEAMI *resumes his stance. Suddenly the high sound of a flute echoes in empty space. He strikes the drum, producing a sharp sound in the distance. He continues to strike the drum rapidly.*)

ZEAMI: What about it then? Did the drum sound?

YOSHITSUGU: Splendid as usual. Who can say that it did not sound?

LADY KUZUNO: There is no mistake. The drum did sound.

ZEAMI (*with a loud laugh*): So you heard a sound? The drum made a sound? I heard something else. I heard Lord Yoshimitsu's laugh. Do you understand? My love for you, my risking my life for that love, all no more than a performance. What for me was death or madness was for him the dance of a butterfly, flirting over a flower. Well, Lord Yoshimitsu. I respectfully decline to perform again.

YOSHITSUGU: I had no idea. I never realized how my father had beaten you down. Well, my father is dead. He looks at you no longer.

LADY KUZUNO: Both of us are free, Zeami. Free from Yoshimitsu.

ZEAMI: Perhaps you can say that you are free. But I, who find my only life in the eyes of the audience . . . I, free from

[66]

what? What an absurdity. How can a fish be free from water? The drum just now. You thought it sounded. Because behind your eyes are the eyes of Lord Yoshimitsu. My skill was forged, sustained by those eyes. Lord Yoshimitsu is not really dead. Even now he stares at me, his gaze unaverted. Kikyō, bring the robe.

(KIKYŌ *leaves*.)

YOSHITSUGU: You have not changed at all, Zeami. You still play the Shadow to my father. How terrifying this is.

ZEAMI (*to himself*): Lord Yoshimitsu, always look at me. For to be looked at can be my only purpose in life.

(KIKYŌ *comes back with the robe*.)

ZEAMI: Here is the robe you gave me as a token of our love, consummated on that one night alone. As long as the eyes of Lord Yoshimitsu live on, the robe will be you, you as you were that night. It will be you that I hold when I embrace this robe. No more than that. For this robe seems more real than you yourself. (*He laughs*.) You see. Your living presence is no longer required. So please go home. For a Shadow can do nothing more than embrace this cast-off skin of yours. For a Shadow, there can be no other way.

(LADY KUZUNO *covers her face*. YOSHITSUGU *supports her*.)

YOSHITSUGU: I see now, Zeami. It is not I who you hate. Nor my brother Yoshimochi. It is our father, Yoshimitsu. And I understand, now, what that old Sorceress said so long ago. About a Shadow that hates the Light.

LADY KUZUNO: Stop, please stop, Zeami. I can bear no more. I too must despise a man who gave your soul such agony. But now you must forgive him. Forgive him, and become again a man. A true human being.

YOSHITSUGU: Zeami. I must apologize to you. You have forced me to finally understand the enormity of the crimes inflicted on you by my father. I apologize, in his

[67]

name and in the name of all those who presume to represent the Light. Zeami. Become a warrior. Or a simple citizen. Free yourself from all this.

ZEAMI: No, Lord Yoshitsugu. I find it unnecessary to accept
your apology. For it was I myself who, ten years ago,
agreed to become a Shadow. I cannot become a warrior,
or an upright citizen. To take pleasure now in such a life
would be to sink into self-contempt. I would finish by
becoming like those who have despised me.

YOSHITSUGU (*laughing hysterically*): You? How absurd! A
Shadow from which the self has been stripped away—
how can you yourself agree to become anything at all?

ZEAMI: Things are as they are.

YOSHITSUGU: And so, as a result, Light itself has its very essence stolen away.

(*The sound of conch-shell trumpets and military drums can be
heard outside the gates.*)

MOTOYOSHI (*behind the scenes*): The attack! They're closing in!

(ZEAMI *quietly closes his eyes.*)

LADY KUZUNO: Then remember this, Zeami. You may have
dispelled your feelings of hatred, but you have sacrificed
the love and devotion of a woman's heart in the process.
Lord Yoshimitsu has crippled many, but you cannot say
that your own hands are clean. Come with me, Lord
Yoshitsugu. I will shelter you. (*Looking into* ZEAMI's *face.*)
A woman who has been shamed fears nothing. For the
present, you may assume that I will protect you.

(LADY KUZUNO *and* YOSHITSUGU *leave.* KIKYŌ *and* ZEAMI, *left
behind, stand hushed.*)

KIKYŌ (*with emotion*): I feel so happy. So happy for you.

ZEAMI: You heard everything then.

KIKYŌ: Surely your wife Tsubaki is waiting for you. Hurry to
her side.

ZEAMI: Tsubaki? Is something the matter?

KIKYŌ (*gasping*): Is something the matter! Is that what you said?

ZEAMI (*as though awakening from a dream, with great gentleness*): Do you mean she's not feeling well?

KIKYŌ: Zeami. (*A pause.*) Then it's not because of your wife that . . . I can't understand. For the sake of art, how can men become so merciless? Why must they become so cruel?

ZEAMI: Is that how you feel? Perhaps I was wrong to let you witness what you did.

KIKYŌ: Perhaps you are right. Today I am going to quit your house and leave your family.

ZEAMI: Please put your mind at rest. Art is a Hell. And I have no intention of dragging you into it.

KIKYŌ: I must leave. I realize there is cruelty everywhere. But I cannot believe that the man I have come to regard as my own father could be so heartless.

ZEAMI (*after a pause*): Kikyō.

KIKYŌ: Yes?

ZEAMI: The drum. Did you hear anything when I struck it?

KIKYŌ: No. I heard nothing at all.

ZEAMI: Is that so? Why, then, fine. You will be able to go wherever you please. You are not caught by Lord Yoshimitsu's eyes. Your own eyes can seek out your own happiness. This is a most auspicious thing. And it may signal the end of me as well. (*He laughs.*)

(*Suddenly* RETAINERS *rush in from every side, their weapons drawn. They surround* KIKYŌ *and* ZEAMI *completely.*)

ZEAMI: Kikyō! That song! Sing it now!

KIKYŌ: The song? Then you don't mind that I sing it?

ZEAMI: Yes! Sing it! Sing it in my place.

KIKYŌ (*singing*):
"I'm glad the nightingale is dead.
I'm glad the flowers fall.

Zeami

Set fire to the universe itself!
I will dance on, madly dance, alone! . . ."
(*As she continues to sing in her artless fashion, the curtain falls.*)

Act Four

The same setting as Act One. Fall, the eleventh month. Several groups of hanging chrysanthemums. Evening. The sun is still red in the sky. Fifteen years have passed since Act Three. ZEAMI *is now almost seventy.*
(*As the curtain rises, he is speaking sharply with an envoy of the Shōgun.* TSUBAKI *sits behind them, quietly.*)

ZEAMI: Go back and tell the Shōgun that no matter how old and decrepit I may be, I refuse to obey such an order. My oldest son Motomasa is heir to the family and to the family traditions. No actor so lacking in skill as my nephew On'ami can possibly be considered for appointment as my successor.

ENVOY: But such is the Shōgun's personal command. He finds nothing to interest him in the art of your son Motomasa. "He may have depth, elegant simplicity, or whatever," the Shōgun said, "but Motomasa thinks all too highly of himself, and he disgusts me."

ZEAMI: I am already quite familiar with that kind of complaint. Such is the excuse my son was given this spring when they took away his position as Master of Music at

[70]

the Kiyotaki Shrine. No doubt that is why I, too, old man that I am, may no longer enter the palace. But in fact, the art of my son is the same as my own. The Shōgun seems to despise everything about the art of our whole Kanze family. So I cannot imagine why the matter of who succeeds me as head of the family should be a matter of such interest to him. The whole thing escapes my understanding.

ENVOY: Because your name, Zeami, still carries with it some reflection of Yoshimitsu himself. And everything that Yoshimitsu possessed, all the Shōguns since that time have wanted to possess as well. First Lord Yoshimochi, now his successor Lord Yoshinori. Everything.

ZEAMI: And if I refuse?

ENVOY: Your whole family will be destroyed. And you will be banished, to a distant island.

ZEAMI: I will never permit On'ami to succeed me. At the least, my younger son Motoyoshi must be chosen.

ENVOY: Lord Zeami, there is nothing you can do to oppose this. Even your sons, whom you have been careful to protect, have deserted you, long ago. Everyone, including the Shōgun, has heard the rumor that both of them are quite prepared to cut their ties with the Kanze family at any time now.

ZEAMI (*after a pause*): Yes, I must admit, there is some truth in what you say. My sons are prepared to desert me. Yet how can I blame them? There seems no hope for any of us in the future.

ENVOY: My duty is a painful one. I feel very deeply for you in the present circumstances. Perhaps, now that I think about it, you were too much favored by Lord Yoshimitsu.

ZEAMI: And that is not all. There is the whole affair with Lord Yoshitsugu. How extraordinary that I should still be living on, fifteen years after his death.

ENVOY: That is true, of course. Yet then, too, you had help. From Lady Kuzuno. Whatever the circumstances, she could be counted on to come to your aid. But she too is dead. Nothing stands between you and your fate.

ZEAMI: Banishment, to an island? I can bear that . . . But my sons . . .

ENVOY: It is no use, Lord Zeami. There is no escaping the inevitable. Either your nephew On'ami is given the position as the head of the Kanze family, or that family will be destroyed. That is, unfortunately, all there is to it. I must return now. I will await your answer. But I urge you, in all sincerity: even in desperation, act with prudence. Have the courage to break your ties with the theater. And let On'ami succeed you. (*The* ENVOY *leaves.*)

(ZEAMI *and* TSUBAKI *regard each other, without speaking. A brief silence.*)

TSUBAKI: How ironic life can be. You and I are finally joined together, as a real couple. But the frost has already fallen. On the chrysanthemums, here in our garden. And, somehow, it has fallen on us as well.

ZEAMI: Don't grumble. It helps nothing.

TSUBAKI: They are all gone now. Everyone. Even Kikyō, who was so dear to us. All. Gone, long since.

ZEAMI: Perhaps a husband and wife are meant to meet twice in their lifetime. At the end, when the sun begins to set, the others take their leave, the tide ebbs away. Suddenly, there we are, quietly facing each other. Perhaps it is at such a moment when marriage truly begins.

TSUBAKI: True, it has been forty years . . . and where have you been, those forty years, I wonder . . . ?

ZEAMI: Forty years. As long as that . . .

TSUBAKI: Is that all you can say? How I have grown weary, waiting for you. I have become an old woman.

ZEAMI: Did you hate me then . . . ?

[72]

TSUBAKI (*with a soft laugh*): It must be twenty years since my body burned with solitary longing. I don't suppose you ever noticed. I hung a bell in our family temple, there in the back. I thought that when my own heart was ready to burst, I would go and strike that bell, to destroy it instead. And yet I'm glad to say that up until now, at least, I've never had to go quite that far.

ZEAMI (*after a pause*): I have been roaming in a strange land. A land where drums that make no sound are heard, where empty robes hold human warmth. Do you despise me? If you must, then I suppose you must. For I myself do not understand what has been the purpose of this strange voyage I have made.

TSUBAKI: But I do.

ZEAMI: What is it then?

TSUBAKI: You left us so that you could appreciate us, your wife and your children. From afar.

ZEAMI (*with a hearty laugh*): Only a woman would say a thing like that.

TSUBAKI (*continuing*): No. I am right. Otherwise, why would you compose plays so filled with longing for family, for wives, and for children? Especially the play you wrote about the cloth-fulling block. To me it seems like a communication from some vague and distant land, addressed to me alone.

ZEAMI: Yes. I put into that play my conception of the feelings of a woman who has been deserted by her husband. But I must confess I never imagined that you yourself had been so touched by what I wrote.

TSUBAKI: There are others too. The play about the heavenly drum, for instance. In that play the father yearns for his son.

ZEAMI: You are right. Yes. I have been a cold husband, a cold father. Perhaps I have yearned for you and my two sons

[73]

all my life. Yearned, at the bottom of my heart, yet understanding so little . . . (*He laughs lightly.*) How absurd all this is. I have asked for nothing more than to live in this frightful world of men, all these forty years. And yet even so, I . . .

TSUBAKI: A wife has her pride, her false pride. No matter what a man may think or do, a woman goes on imagining that he does it only for her sake. But you must not blame me for feeling this way. Without a crutch like this, how can any woman hope to go on living her life?

ZEAMI: There are many kinds of crutches. And they are all indispensable. I wanted to find out something else. I wanted to see how far I could go on living my life without a crutch of any kind.

TSUBAKI: And all that time your sons and I have lived on with no one, no one to turn to.

ZEAMI (*turning away, in pain*): And now, Motomasa and Motoyoshi are both prepared to abandon their father.

TSUBAKI: Yet how much Motomasa loves you! Just look at the plays the boy has written. The one about the ghost of the child at the Sumida river. Or the play about the frail priest. These plays are filled with the voice of a child, seeking his parent.

ZEAMI: To your ears, all drama seems to represent the cries of your family.

TSUBAKI: But for all those years you have only been able to communicate with us through your plays. Only in my ears have I been able to maintain a sense of my ghostly family.

ZEAMI: And, as I awaken from this dream, my real family seems nowhere to be found. It exists no longer. (*He gives a hollow laugh.*)

(MOTOMASA *and* MOTOYOSHI *enter.*)

MOTOMASA: So then, Father. The time has come for us to part from you. You will not see us again in this life.

ZEAMI: I know that. You leave so as to make me suffer all the more. So that your father, so unworthy of you, will harbor his remorse until he dies.

MOTOMASA: That is not true. Father, we are not abandoning you. We are abandoning the theater.

ZEAMI: Abandoning the theater?

MOTOMASA: And is this not a triumph? The perfect revenge? The theater has made a plaything of you. It has stolen from you your own humanity. We hate the theater. And how many others have been treated no differently from you? And all of them for the same reasons.

ZEAMI: Do not exaggerate the misery that is past. I realize that I may have made your lives lonely. And your mother's. But . . .

MOTOMASA: I was not speaking about that.

ZEAMI: I know. You are grumbling over your present misfortune. And you are right. There is no doubt that for our whole family the winds of autumn are blowing in earnest. But the reason for that has nothing to do with the theater.

MOTOMASA: Then what, or who, is responsible? The present Shōgun, Yoshinori? Or Yoshimochi before him? Or are you trying to say that it was Lord Yoshimitsu himself after all?

ZEAMI: It is certainly no use to go into all that now. Suffice to say that the theater gave me a stronghold from which I was able to attack all those men.

MOTOMASA: A stronghold? Rather a shackle and chains. Because of the theater, you fled those battles when you should have stayed to fight. Fifteen years ago Lord Yoshitsugu had the courage to face his own shame. And to take his own life. Even he, who feared death so much. When have you, Father, ever shown such resolve?

ZEAMI (*after a pause*): Then, you intend to go . . . and die?

MOTOMASA: I will go to Ochi, in Yamato. There is a battle

raging there now. The Ochi family will certainly be defeated. And they will surely die making a brave and a
final defense. I will join with those doomed warriors and
earn a noble death.

TSUBAKI: Motomasa! What can you possibly owe to the Ochi
family? You have no ties to them at all.

ZEAMI: Explain yourself. If you have some kind of foolish
sympathy for the underdog, better give up the whole
thing at once.

MOTOMASA: You are right. I have no ties with them at all. I
have never even come in contact with them. How could I
have any sympathy for them? Any battle, anywhere, will
do. I only seek an occasion when my life or death can be
determined by my own strength.

ZEAMI: You want to become a warrior then, Motomasa?

MOTOMASA: I'm tired of playing a Shadow. I know that much.

ZEAMI: Go on.

MOTOMASA: For a warrior, his life is in his deeds. He defeats
a worthy enemy, and his proper prize is his own life that
he has saved. Whatever others may say, the warrior can
assert this much. He takes one head in battle. Two
heads. So his existence grows all the more real, all the
richer, all the deeper. I envy this.

ZEAMI: Yes. I too have felt that same envy.

MOTOMASA: But what of us? An actor's life is the audience.
And his appeal for them. My own feelings about what I
do have no reality for them. And so no genuine reality at
all.

ZEAMI: You are right. And I have always told you the same
thing: if the eyes of the audience are clouded over, you
must devise something to suit those eyes as well.

MOTOMASA: I detest that necessity. I detest it with all the
force of my being. There is nothing so capricious in this
whole world as an audience. They applaud, even when I
myself cannot discover what they find pleasing; then,

before I know it, they lose their enthusiasm altogether. I do not believe I have ever received what I would call proper applause. Not in all my career. And yet the only life I possess as a man lies in that applause.

(ZEAMI *has begun to smile during this speech; now, he laughs aloud.*)

MOTOMASA: Father, what can you possibly find amusing in all this?

ZEAMI: Isn't it frightening? Isn't it all frightening, Motomasa? You are trying to stand in a terrible swamp that has no bottom. Every human being depends on his sense of self. But that crutch is not there for you. Because, from the very beginning, you have entrusted it to others. Yet you yourself have never believed in those others. Not for an instant.

MOTOMASA: But Father, don't you feel any shame? To be satisfied with an existence like that?

ZEAMI: I did not intend merely to be satisfied. I made a conscious choice. The choice to lead an existence like that.

MOTOMASA: I remember your telling me all that before. But such logic is merely an excuse.

ZEAMI: An excuse? For what?

MOTOMASA: Lady Kuzuno. You surely haven't forgotten about her.

ZEAMI (*after a pause*): Lady Kuzuno is dead. Long ago.

MOTOMASA: She loved you, Father. And your attitude sent her, insane, to her own death. Excuse me, Mother. I must speak of this. Because that was the first time, fifteen years ago, when my brother and I lost confidence in our father. On that cold winter's day. When our father spurned that poor woman who went down on her knees before him. You were afraid, afraid of what might happen afterwards to your precious theater. And so you turned your back on her. In cowardice.

ZEAMI: Nonsense! I did not permit what could not be permitted.

MOTOMASA: In order to dispel your own self-indulgent bitterness, you never hesitated to trample on that poor woman's very soul. I cannot find such behavior acceptable.

ZEAMI: You are still a young man, Motomasa. At your age, it is always more pleasant to forgive rather than to condemn.

MOTOMASA: Condemn, did you say? Do you mean poor Lady Kuzuno, who had no one at all to whom she could turn?

ZEAMI: My enemy has always been invisible. Yet invisible, Lord Yoshimitsu is everywhere. In her heart. And in mine.

MOTOMASA: Of course, Father. Your enemy is the theater, the theater that occupies your very soul.

ZEAMI: Motoyoshi. Do you intend to seek your death as well?

MOTOYOSHI: Father, I plan to renounce the world and enter the priesthood.

ZEAMI: Are you so weary of life then?

MOTOYOSHI: No, that's not it. But I must confess that I am weary of your passion for this world.

ZEAMI: My passion for this world?

MOTOMASA: For sixty years you have harbored your suspicions and your griefs. It is this which wearies me of this world. Even the enormous authority of Lord Yoshimitsu himself, whom you took to be your Light, seems at best only a Shadow before the transcendent Light of the Buddha. And you, Father, who thought to defy the Light, became in the end only the Shadow of a Shadow. How lacking in any human dignity. How miserable. Behind a screen of elegance and beauty, your theater harbors all the malice, all the envy of the world. I have grown weary of it.

[78]

(*Just then, at some distance, a woman's voice can be heard singing. The sound is bright and clear, much like the voice of* KIKYŌ.)

MOTOMASA: Before, the songs the actors sang must have been bright and cheerful. Joyful, the kind of songs that people might have used in worship. Listen to that artless melody. They must have been just like that.

(*The song can be heard distinctly now. It is* HAGI's *song. Yet, sung in this fashion, it suggests a brighter emotion.*)

    "I'm glad the nightingale is dead.
    I'm glad the flowers fall.
    Set fire to the universe itself!
    I will dance on, madly dance, alone!"

ZEAMI: That . . . that is Kikyō's song. Do you think she has come back?

MOTOMASA: If it is Kikyō, she must be a woman of more than thirty now. If there's any resemblance in the voices, it is more likely to be her daughter.

MOTOYOSHI: There's no resemblance at all. The words are the same, but now the song seems bright and gay. That melody must have passed from one person to another. Before, the song was heavy with malice. Now all that has been washed away.

(*Now the song is sung by three women together.*)

MOTOYOSHI: Now they sing it together. Before, that would have been impossible. A song of bitterness must be sung alone.

ZEAMI: The sound has faded. Can you still hear it?

MOTOYOSHI: Yes. And before it disappears completely I must take my leave as well.

TSUBAKI: Where will you go? And will you let us hear from you?

MOTOYOSHI: I will become a mendicant priest. I will follow that song everywhere. We will surely meet again, somewhere, at some time. Perhaps by next summer's Festival

[79]

of Lanterns, dances of my devising will be popular here in the capital. So then. I respectfully take my leave. (MOTO-YOSHI *turns and leaves the stage.*)

TSUBAKI: Wait, Motoyoshi. I want you to take something with you as a memento. At least a robe, perhaps . . . (*She hurries off the stage.*)

MOTOMASA: Now I, too, Father, will take my leave. While Mother is gone. I cannot bear to witness her sorrow any longer. I will go before she comes back.

ZEAMI (*with sudden intensity*): Motomasa. Live! And come back to us alive!

MOTOMASA: I do not see how that could be. (*He starts to leave.*) Of course, if you, Father . . .

ZEAMI: If I what . . . what, Motomasa?

MOTOMASA: If you promise to abandon the theater . . . throw it over completely . . .

ZEAMI: If I throw it over . . . you will return?

MOTOMASA: I plan to pass the night at the inn at Ujitahara, not far from the capital. After you have thought the matter over carefully, send word as quickly as you can. I will return to you. I will return, and you and I can farm the land.

ZEAMI: Do you think you will enjoy working in the fields?

MOTOMASA: As a farmer, you determine your own value: a sheaf of rice you have gathered, a cluster of turnips you have picked. Nothing anyone else may say can matter. You know what represents your own accomplishment. Applause is not involved. What you produce serves as proof enough of your existence. Father. Join with me. Farm the land.

ZEAMI: I see. Go then.

MOTOMASA: Very well. But I will be waiting. And may the news you send be good. (MOTOMASA *leaves the stage, which quickly darkens.*)

ZEAMI: Tsubaki. Tsubaki? Where have you gone? Tsubaki!

(*The* OLD SORCERESS *appears behind the shrubs in the garden.*)

ZEAMI: Tsubaki! Everything before me seems so dark. Bring some light. Tsubaki! Some light!

OLD SORCERESS: Are you afraid, Lord Zeami? You cannot become a Shadow altogether. Do you understand now, Lord Zeami? What happens when you try to become a Shadow?

ZEAMI: Old woman! Is that you? Where are you? Wait! (*He goes toward the shrubs, but the* OLD SORCERESS *disappears.* TSUBAKI *now stands there instead; the stage brightens.*)

TSUBAKI: Did you ask for some light? But the sun has not yet set . . .

ZEAMI: Tsubaki. I will abandon . . . I will abandon the theater.

TSUBAKI: What do you mean?

ZEAMI: I shall pass my title as Head of the Kanze family on to my nephew On'ami. Tomorrow I will gather the whole family together. We will begin our work in the fields.

TSUBAKI: You mean that you will abandon . . . everything?

ZEAMI: Yes. Exactly that. This means too that, from tomorrow morning, you will be a farmer's wife.

TSUBAKI (*after a long pause*): I will take away that bell I hung in the garden. It represented for me all the suffering a woman can know. How happy I am that I have never had to ring it. I shall pay obeisance to the bell and let it sink into the depths of the lake.

(*Suddenly* ON'AMI *enters.*)

ON'AMI: Uncle! I heard what you said. That I might head the Kanze house. Or, could I somehow have misunderstood?

ZEAMI: Were you hiding, listening to what we were saying?

ON'AMI: This is my house now. There is nothing now that I can't do, if I choose to. I shall become like you, Uncle, as you were when Lord Yoshimitsu was still alive.

ZEAMI: That makes you happy, I suppose.

ON'AMI: You should know the answer to that, better than

[81]

anyone else. With the world at his feet, only a fool would feel any regret.

ZEAMI: And you feel no humiliation at all.

ON'AMI: Humiliation? Beacuse of what?

ZEAMI: Over your conduct at this very moment.

ON'AMI: What nonsense. When you feel happy, you ought to be able to say so, and openly. A sour disposition is no help to anyone these days.

ZEAMI: Get out of here. You shall have the title. But I never want to see you here again.

ON'AMI: Don't be so quick-tempered. You may feel you dislike me. But you must admit that I have always done my best to understand and carry out your teachings.

ZEAMI: My teachings!

ON'AMI: Of course. Our art lies in the eyes of our spectators. I understand you perfectly. For an actor, the self is a useless impediment. A performance must be conceived in terms of pleasing the audience. That's what you said . . .

ZEAMI (*puffing*): What nonsense! He's painted a comic portrait of me. Did you hear him, Tsubaki? He's reduced me to a caricature!

ON'AMI: Uncle! You should speak more prudently to the man who will head the whole Kanze family.

ZEAMI: You've said quite enough. Go away. Go home.

ON'AMI: I have no intention of leaving. I know very well that these past few years you have been writing down all the secret traditions of your art, and in great detail. And by rights that document belongs to me now.

ZEAMI: By rights? What does that mean? Besides, there is no such document.

ON'AMI: You've hidden your writings. I know. You have discussed everything there, from mimicry to the secrets of the dance. You call your account "Secret Teachings on

[82]

the Transmission of the Flower." Everything is written out in detail. Well. I want you to give all of that to me.

ZEAMI: The Shōgun is your teacher. You have nothing to learn from me.

ON'AMI: There is no use in discussing the matter. Give me what you've written.

ZEAMI: And . . . if I decline to do so?

ON'AMI: That would be the same as refusing to make me your successor. For refusing to obey the wishes of the Shōgun, you will be banished. To some distant island. Immediately.

ZEAMI: Wretched coward!

ON'AMI: Call me whatever names you please. I am utterly indifferent. But I am waiting for your answer. Well, Uncle, what about it?

ZEAMI (*pauses; then, forcefully*): I refuse.

(*For an instant,* TSUBAKI *is unable to move. Then she runs off stage in great agitation.*)

ON'AMI (*gently*): Uncle, you can gain nothing by your stubbornness. It is very unpleasant for me to have to take this attitude with you. But now, someone must play this part too. For the sake of the theater you have created. If your writings should disappear, our whole art would be lost. Everything you have struggled to achieve in your own lifetime would be buried along with you. So then. Hand everything over to me. I promise you, Uncle, that I will pass your writings down to later generations.

ZEAMI: I refuse. If these writings were something I could give to someone like you, I might as well burn them here and now.

ON'AMI: What are you worried about? For the others, later, you will not seem to have been the weak one. I will have been the villain. But the secrets of your art must be safely preserved. Come now. Hand them over.

[83]

ZEAMI: Be quiet! (*Screaming.*) That will do. Do you understand?

(*Suddenly the sound of a bell shattering fills the stage.*)

ON'AMI: Uncle! Listen to that. That bell has been still for
  twenty years. Now it sounds. Do you want to ring out
  the deaths of all your family?

ZEAMI: Leave me! Leave me, I tell you.

ON'AMI: Splendid! But Uncle, after all, you don't have the
  temperament to kill another man. Still, you are stubborn.
  It is that same stubbornness that drives Motomasa to the
  battlefield.

ZEAMI: No. My own hands have long been soiled. Do you
  think I felt nothing when I cast Lady Kuzuno aside?

ON'AMI: How many? How many people do you intend to sac-
  rifice before you have satisfied yourself?

ZEAMI (*fiercely*): Ask Yoshimitsu.

ON'AMI: Uncle. Do you still bear such a grudge against Lord
  Yoshimitsu? Men must play many roles. After all, is it so
  bad to be born a Shadow? Take my case. I am happy,
  from the bottom of my heart. I am all too pleased to
  play that part. I want to do my best to give a performance that will find favor in the eyes of my audience.
  And is there anything humiliating in that? To forget
  yourself, to concern yourself only with the eyes of those
  who watch you—why, every man who has ever been in
  love knows this happiness.

ZEAMI (*with a slight laugh*): On'ami. I realize that I am delighted that you have come. Because now, thanks to you,
  I have found a real reason to become a Shadow again.
  Lord Yoshimitsu has been dead for thirty years now.
  And old resentments tend to fade. One begins to weary
  of one's preoccupations. The temptation to finish out the
  rest of one's life as quietly as possible is very strong . . .
  But today, Yoshimitsu has flung down his challenge to
  me again, On'ami. He has created a fraud like you to

sport with me, his Shadow, once again. To mock the very idea of a Shadow . . . Yoshimitsu is still alive. He plots to fill the world with false Shadows and bury me forever. Well. Be careful, Yoshimitsu. Zeami is still alive as well. A Shadow is always a Shadow, until the very end.

(TSUBAKI's *bell continues to ring, sometimes strongly, sometimes faintly; it dies out, then begins again. As* ZEAMI *finishes speaking, a temple bell begins to sound, as if in response, tolling the sunset hour. The stage fills with the sound.* ZEAMI *is bathed in the red light of the setting sun.*)

Curtain

Epilogue

1432. The eighth month. The afternoon of the Festival of Lanterns. A street in Kyoto. Groups of outcasts are squatting here and there. From stage left enters a Government OFFICIAL (*the* ENVOY *of Act Four can play this role as well), from stage right* ON'AMI. *Each is accompanied by several* RETAINERS.

ON'AMI: Was he there?
OFFICIAL: No. And you?
ON'AMI: I couldn't find him. But I know I saw him around here somewhere.

OFFICIAL: Well, he seems to have slipped away . . .

ON'AMI: You think he's escaped?

OFFICIAL: Yes. Zeami must have heard very quickly about the decision to banish him to the island of Sado.

ON'AMI: No, no. Even if my uncle manages to elude us for the moment, he's no longer at an age when he can summon the necessary strength to make an escape. And now, especially, since he's heard the rumor that his oldest son Motomasa was killed near Ise. He must surely have lost all his strength. He is certainly still here in the capital. Probably wandering around somewhere.

OFFICIAL: Do you think that Motomasa is really dead? Today is the Festival of Lanterns. His soul might be returning again to this world, for the first time.

ON'AMI: Perhaps I will have a chance to meet his ghost then, wandering around somewhere or other. (*He laughs lightly.*)

OFFICIAL: Do you have a bad conscience about all this?

ON'AMI: I? What did I do? Sink, swim, it's all a question of fate.

OFFICIAL: And your fate seems an auspicious one, Lord On'ami. What's more, you know what you want.

ON'AMI: You need courage to confront good fortune. Far more than to face adversity. Like standing at the top of that pagoda over there: the eyes of a weak man will spin in his head.

OFFICIAL: I see what you mean. Perhaps then Zeami will have no need for all those secret writings of his. Perhaps he'll give them to you after all.

ON'AMI: My uncle? I cannot imagine that he would give them to me.

OFFICIAL: If only he had. The need for that terrible judgment he received today would never have come about.

(*In the distance a group of women can be heard singing; their song is accompanied by flutes, drums, and bells.*)

[86]

"I'm glad the nightingale is dead.
I'm glad the flowers fall.
Set fire to the universe itself!"
                    (*etc.*)

OFFICIAL: Oh! Listen to that song.

ON'AMI: They must be singing for the Festival of Lanterns.

OFFICIAL: There is an epidemic of dancing these days. Recently there was a huge group assembled at one of the temples near here. Hundreds, thousands, it seemed. I heard that because of their cries and the stamping of their feet, the Great Hall itself began to shake.

ON'AMI: Such turbulent behavior is very disturbing. The Shōgun himself must have been concerned.

OFFICIAL: No, no. After all, it's only dancing. Let them dance. It will keep them too busy for anything else.

ON'AMI: But there are even worse things than the dancing. Don't you know that the townspeople have taken to giving performances in imitation of our own? They are of an extreme vulgarity, and they must be stopped.

OFFICIAL: Actually . . .

ON'AMI: "Actually . . ." What do you mean by that?

OFFICIAL: Those amateur performances are often criticized, but in fact they are always most interesting. They are colorful and simple to understand. And, Lord On'ami, if you will excuse me for saying so, they resemble in many ways your own style of performance.

ON'AMI: I see. You mean to tell me that the taste of the Shōgun himself is no different from that of the farmers. That both enjoy the same dances?

OFFICIAL: Certainly not! I would never dare even to suggest such an outrageous thing.

ON'AMI: I wonder. In any case, it would hardly do to have that rumor spread about. All the more reason to have those amateur performances suppressed.

OFFICIAL (*avoiding the subject*): Look! The dancers are heading this way. The streets will be swarming with people. We must hurry to find Lord Zeami.

ON'AMI: Yes, we must go. I don't want to find my uncle collapsed in the road.

OFFICIAL: You are right. He's got to be sent off to his place of exile. And without any delay.

ON'AMI: You look this way.

OFFICIAL: And you, Lord On'ami, go over there. (*They nod goodbye and go off in opposite directions.*)

(*Eventually the singing voices grow louder, and a group of* DANCERS *bursts onto the stage. As many as possible should be provided in order to create a strong effect. Their appearance is strange, splendid; some wear curious costumes, and others are masked. The girls among them are healthy and overflowing with sensual charm. At the edge of the group appears* MOTOYOSHI *who seems to be leading them. The group remains in the center of the stage, dacing wildly. Among them one stands out*—KAEDE, *the daughter of* KIKYŌ. *She is completely absorbed in her dancing.*)

CHORUS: "Shall I tell you how I feel?"

(*The refrain rises like the wind. Then the group begins to ebb away toward stage right. As it does so,* ZEAMI *enters from stage left. His hair is completely white. He walks unsteadily.*)

ZEAMI (*in a strained voice*): Motoyoshi. Motoyoshi! Wait! Don't you hear me, Motoyoshi?

CHORUS: "Shall I tell you how I feel?"

ZEAMI (*screaming*): Motoyoshi! Motoyoshi!

(*The group of* DANCERS *seems to push* MOTOYOSHI *toward* ZEAMI. *It returns to fill about one third of the stage.*)

ZEAMI: Oh! It's you, isn't it, Motoyoshi? Motoyoshi! (ZEAMI *and* MOTOYOSHI *face each other, about six feet apart. The noise of the* DANCERS *grows fainter.*) There is one thing . . . one thing . . . that I must tell you. Your brother . . . Motomasa . . . he is dead. (*A pause.*) And what a fool he was. Weak. He was too weak. A fool. But Motoyoshi. You must see to it that a service is said in his memory.

(MOTOYOSHI *is silent for a moment. Then he screams out to the* DANCERS.)

MOTOYOSHI: Dance! Dance on! And sing!

CHORUS: "Shall I tell you how I feel?"

(*The* DANCERS, *singing at the tops of their voices, spill out into the center of the stage.* ZEAMI *is pushed about by them but tries desperately to get as close as possible to* MOTOYOSHI.)

ZEAMI: Motoyoshi . . . you too, my son? You too would leave your father . . .

MOTOYOSHI: Dance! Sing! I don't know this whining old fool. Get out of the way! Dance!

(*The* DANCERS *surround* ZEAMI, *pushing him about.*)

ZEAMI: You are a spoiled child! How deplorable this all is! Are you still so petulant then? (ZEAMI *manages to get closer to* MOTOYOSHI, *but just as he comes close he is pushed over and trampled on by the frantic* DANCERS.) Ah!

MOTOYOSHI: Wait!

(*The* DANCERS *see what has happened and quickly become calm.*)

ZEAMI (*incoherently*): So. So, Motoyoshi . . . you are what I say: a spoiled child, after all. Yes you are. You are weak. You. And your brother Motomasa too. Well, go right on. Now, yes . . . Dance, go on, dance.(ZEAMI *faints. The* DANCERS *slowly retire. Suddenly, the sound of a tolling bell is heard; the stage darkens. The* DANCERS *leave.* ZEAMI *is alone. The sound of the* DANCERS' *feet soon vanishes as well.*)

(*The sound of the bell continues to reverberate. In the darkness appears the ghost of* MOTOMASA.)

MOTOMASA'S GHOST: Stop that the ringing! That bell is surely at the bottom of the lake, yet it echoes, even from the depths of the water. And I cannot sleep. Stop it. Oh, please stop the bell.

[89]

Zeami

ZEAMI (*still on the ground*): Give up then, Motomasa. Didn't you achieve your wish after all? You had no long life to suffer through as a Shadow. You became Light. And like Light you have faded.

MOTOMASA'S GHOST: But Father, why is it I cannot sleep? To shine, to fade, what could be simpler? Indeed, it was all too simple, and I took no pleasure from it. You, Father, you suffered the life of a Shadow and seemed a coward. Yet it is you who, after all, were the most admirable.

ZEAMI: You are raving . . . raving, my son. Well then, rave on. I shall take the image of your melancholy figure and put it on the stage. You shall serve as my model for the apparition of a defeated warrior.

MOTOMASA'S GHOST: Father, Father, it is for that very reason that I cannot sleep. I must wander in the world until this very bell floats up to the surface of the lake. Stop its ringing, Father. Stop its ringing.

(*The sound of a drum fills the air; the sound of the bell fades. As the sound of the drum continues, the ghost of* MOTOMASA *disappears and the ghost of* YOSHITSUGU *quietly replaces it.*)

YOSHITSUGU'S GHOST: Stop! Stop the drum! Wherever I flee, I hear it. No matter how I stop up my ears, that sound follows me. Stop! Let Yoshitsugu sleep, even a little. Let me rest.

ZEAMI: What do you expect from a Shadow? As long as Light remains in the world, the Shadow Drum must continue sounding by itself.

YOSHITSUGU'S GHOST: This is not how I had planned it, Zeami. Quite the opposite. As long as you, the Shadow, live on, as long as you reflect what we have been, those of us who represent the Light can have no rest. Give it up! I am tired. So tired.

(*The gloomy laughter of* YOSHIMITSU *pours out from below the ground.*)

[90]

YOSHITSUGU'S GHOST: Do you hear that, Zeami? My father, Yoshimitsu, too, can have no rest. He sees how you have made manifest, and without pity, his every act. He cannot sleep.

(*The sound of the drum drowns out* YOSHIMITSU'S *laughter.*)

YOSHITSUGU'S GHOST: Give it up. Give it up, please. Until the damask drum turns into a real one, I may never rest. Have pity on me, Zeami.

(*The wheels of a passing oxcart are heard; the drum fades. The ghost of* YOSHITSUGU *disappears, to be replaced by the ghost of* LADY KUZUNO.)

LADY KUZUNO'S GHOST: You must stop my cart, Zeami. Stop my cart. It circles around, around, always passing by your gate. Years, so many years have gone by, and I have never left this terrible cart.

ZEAMI: I cannot forget. Once, twenty-five years ago, you left your cart. I shall always remember how you looked, then.

LADY KUZUNO'S GHOST: I pay heavily for that one burst of pride. I may never leave this cart again for all eternity. But now, Zeami, now you, at least, must forgive me.

ZEAMI: You are so radiantly beautiful, Lady Kuzuno. May you stay always as you are, for all eternity, and men will call you Beauty itself.

LADY KUZUNO'S GHOST: I am wretched and ugly, Lord Zeami. Do you think I am beautiful? Your words strike terror in my heart. The sin, the guilt I thought would vanish with my death now reveals itself in my every aspect. And you call it Beauty. Ah, you must stop the cart for me, Lord Zeami. You must. Until you do, neither I nor Lord Yoshimitsu, who placed me in it, can rest.

(YOSHIMITSU'S *melancholy laughter sounds again, and the ghost of* LADY KUZUNO *disappears.*)

(*Slowly the stage brightens.* MOTOYOSHI *kneels before* ZEAMI, *who is still on the ground.* KAEDE *stands a short distance from them.* MOTOYOSHI *lifts his father in his arms.*)

[91]

Zeami

MOTOYOSHI: Father. Father? Are you yourself again? It is Motoyoshi, Father. Let me help you. We'll go home again, now. Together.

ZEAMI: Motoyoshi. Is it really you then? Really you?

MOTOYOSHI: Father. Before, what happened . . .

ZEAMI: Say nothing. It is I who must speak now. Those dances. What were they? Something you thought up, I suppose . . . but I was disappointed. They . . .

MOTOYOSHI: You will never change, will you father? Not until the end of your days. Those dances you saw were created for a festival. Not for the theater. They are not to be watched. They exist for the pleasure of those who dance.

ZEAMI: I see . . .

MOTOYOSHI: These dances are not art. It does not matter how they look to others. It's like farm work, working with your hands. You do the dances for yourself.

ZEAMI: What's all this? Are you lecturing me?

MOTOYOSHI: You, Father, are the Shadow. One Shadow is enough. These dances will bring Light to the whole country.

ZEAMI: Very well. But the Shadow is still alive. He cannot die as long as Yoshimitsu's eyes are open.

MOTOYOSHI: What remains of Yoshimitsu's Light will fade in tomorrow morning's sun.

ZEAMI: Good. I admire your spirit. But be careful. You must not become another Yoshimitsu yourself.

(ON'AMI, *the* OFFICIAL, *and their* RETAINERS *enter.*)

ON'AMI: So you are here, Uncle. After all.

ZEAMI: My caricature appears again. Yoshimitsu creates one imitation after another, hoping to dissipate the power of the Shadow. Never mind. In five hundred years, in six hundred years, this true Shadow will still remain in the world.

OFFICIAL: Lord Zeami. I bring a command from the Shōgun. Because of the impropriety of your recent actions, you are banished, to the island of Sado.

[92]

MOTOYOSHI: What is this?

ZEAMI: My recent actions, you say? What an absurdity. Well then, On'ami. My writings that you seem so anxious to have. You will find them with my son-in-law, Komparu Zenchiku. He is the one who understands my art the best. He is a bit argumentative, true enough. But a good person in his way. And he might well show them to you. Of course, you'll have to treat him very gently. And behave with proper deference.

ON'AMI: You see? It's just this kind of attitude that has enraged the Shōgun. You have disregarded my express wishes by giving everything to that upstart actor Zenchiku. At some point I know I'll see them. Why do you follow so unprofitable a course?

ZEAMI: I realize now that I have never once seen the Northern Seas. How nice it would be to go off and see Sado Island for a while.

ON'AMI: However old you grow, you still enjoy making others detest you. (ON'AMI *leaves the stage.*)

MOTOYOSHI: Father. To avoid all this trouble, why didn't you destroy what you had written?

ZEAMI: If I did that, all that I have created would perish with me.

MOTOYOSHI: If you leave your secrets to men like On'ami, do you think your art will be protected?

ZEAMI (*with a melancholy laugh*): My son. You are still young. (*He stands quietly, reflecting.*) You do not understand, do you? I have laid a trap. For now on, many who try to understand what I have done will be caught themselves. Mediocre talents will be seduced by words and will reproduce merely the form. Those who are adventuresome will rebel and will destroy that form. Those who have talent will be drowned in their own talent. I have provided a stumbling block for all pretenders, that should last for many hundreds of years. I will always be there to confront them.

MOTOMASA: But for how long? Father. For how long must your curse continue?

ZEAMI: For as long as Yoshimitsu lives, Zeami cannot die. Good-natured Zenchiku has in his grasp a trap that will ensnare all those who practice my art. Forever! It's a bad trick that I am playing, Motomasa. The last one of my life. (*He tries to laugh, but the pain stops him. He finally collapses on the ground.* MOTOYOSHI *frantically tries to help him up.*)

OFFICIAL: His retribution has come. Retribution for his willfulness. Say there! Bring something to carry him on. Hurry!

(*The* RETAINERS *rush off stage. In answer to their cries for help, several* OUTCASTS *enter, carrying a long window-shutter.*)

ZEAMI (*quietly*): Motomasa. Who is she? That young girl there.

MOTOMOSA: She is Kikyō's daughter.

ZEAMI: Kikyō's daughter? Then she must be Hagi's granddaughter.

KAEDE: Sir, my name is Kaede. I was lucky enough to be rescued, just as I was about to be sold as a prostitute. I was saved by your son, Motoyoshi.

ZEAMI: Kaede. What do you know of your mother? Or your grandmother?

KAEDE (*brightly*): Oh, nothing. Nothing at all.

ZEAMI: Is that so? Then, you can know nothing of me.

KAEDE: You are right. I know nothing of you. And I am the one who trampled on you a few moments ago. How can I dare ask you to forgive me?

ZEAMI: What you trampled underfoot was a body that served to contain all that willfulness of mine for more than seventy years. You are the only one who really has the right to step on me.

OFFICIAL: Better not try to speak, Lord Zeami. (*He motions to the* RETAINERS. *The* OUTCASTS *place* ZEAMI *on the shutter.*)

MOTOYOSHI: Father, I had no wish to cause your death. The dancers were advancing; there was no way to prevent them from trampling you underfoot.

ZEAMI (*sternly*): Motoyoshi. I want you to follow the same path I have taken. Tell me that you will.

MOTOYOSHI (*shaking his head vigorously, as though to fling the thought away*): Sing, Kaede. I want you to sing.

(KAEDE *is unable to move. She does not sing.*)

ZEAMI (*gently*): Sing. Sing for my sake then. Just for me. Sing that song that still remains, from thirty years before.

(*The* OUTCASTS *lift up the shutter for* ZEAMI.)

(KAEDE *begins to sing softly, in a clear and happy voice.*)
"I'm glad the nightingale is dead.
I'm glad the flowers fall.
Set fire to the universe itself . . ."

ZEAMI: For thirty years, too, there is a dance that I have been waiting to do. (*Delirious now.*) Hagi! Dance! I will dance too!

(*The* OUTCASTS *begin to carry* ZEAMI *away, as if it were his funeral.* KAEDE *still follows along, singing her song. Just as they are leaving the stage,* MOTOYOSHI *calls out.*)

MOTOYOSHI: Sing! Dance! With everything that is in you!

(*The* CHORUS *responds, like a rushing wind.*)

CHORUS: "Shall I tell you how I feel?"

(*The stage bursts with* DANCERS. *A riot of color and motion. At some point* KAEDE *is separated from* ZEAMI *and is swept into the middle of the dance.* ZEAMI, *on his stretcher, disappears into the swirling crowd.*)

Curtain

Sanetomo

Originally published in Japanese as *Sanetomo shuppan*
(Tokyo: Shinchō-sha)
Copyright © 1973 Masakazu Yamazaki

Sanetomo was first produced in 1973 in Tokyo by the *Te no kai* troupe, when it received an award from the National Arts Festival.

The first English language production was in April 1976.

Characters*

MINAMOTO SANETOMO, The Third Kamakura Shōgun
HŌJŌ MASAKO, Sanetomo's mother, wife of Minamoto Yoritomo (now deceased)
HŌJŌ YOSHITOKI, Sanetomo's uncle, Masako's younger brother
KUGYŌ, Sanetomo's nephew
AZUSA, Sanetomo's wife
MIURA YOSHIMURA, a warrior
WADA YOSHIMORI, a warrior
ŌE HIROMOTO, a civil official of the Kamakura Government
CHEN HO-CH'ING, a craftsman from China
WADA TANENAGA, nephew of Wada Yoshimori (a non-speaking role)
A ghostly FIGURE
VOICES
SAMURAI 1
SAMURAI 2
Several other SAMURAI
WARRIORS 1, 2, 3, 4, and 5
Various other WARRIORS, ARTISANS, and WORKMEN, all male
ACROBATS
An INFANT

*Persons mentioned in the play but who do not appear are: Minamoto Yoriie, Sanetomo's older brother, the father of Kugyō; Minamoto Yoritomo, a famous general, and father of Yoriie and Sanetomo; and Hōjō Tokimasa, Sanetomo's grandfather, and father of Masako and Yoshitoki.

Act One

Above the stage floor is mounted another acting level, a platform forming the large flat center portion with two lower areas surrounding it on either side. The platform is divided into various blocks, and depending on the appropriate change of scene, the shape of the area can be altered accordingly. On and around the platforms are scattered large boxes that can serve as chairs and footstools; above the platform are two large poles, thicker than the span of a man's arm. Their upper reaches rise as though soaring far higher than the top of the state.

All of these stage fittings are colored black or dark brown; as a setting for them, there is a white open space, which, depending on the occasion, can be colored with light in a wide variety of shades. When necessary, a few realistic bits of decor may be added, but such effects should be held to an absolute minimum.

The costumes of the actors are basically ordinary contemporary clothes that might be worn at a rehearsal, over which are worn various robes that suggest, in an abstract fashion, Japanese medieval dress.

Scene One

(*As the curtain rises, one pole rises up on stage left, and behind it, considerably to stage right, rises the second; the sky behind is dyed a fantastic indigo blue. The front of the platform is facing stage left, its tapering point a kind of ladder, giving the effect of the prow of a ship extending toward the audience. Rigging is*

[99]

*strung about from the top of the stage around the platform, and,
at the first pillar, about six feet off the ground, is attached a yardarm wrapped in white sail.)*

VOICES: Sanetomo, Sanetomo!
Sanetomo, Sanetomo, Sanetomo!

*(VOICES well up like a chorus from the obscurity below the plat-
form. As if in response, a strong white light illuminates the first
pole; in the circle of light, the figure of SANETOMO is seen, his legs
crossed, sitting on the rigging. He has a short beard on his chin,
and his long hair is combed to the back. He is a young man of
twenty-two or twenty-three. He is wearing a hunting cloak as
well as a generalized costume; he toys with a ball for* kemari—*a
kind of ancient football. He dangles both his feet, in carefree
mood; but his eyes quietly regard a point in the distant sky and do
not move.)*

VOICES: Sanetomo, Sanetomo, Sanetomo! *(As the various
VOICES whisper out of the darkness, the two areas beside the
platform begin to fill with a dim, yellowish light. Here all the
other characters in the play—*MASAKO, HŌJŌ YOSHITOKI,
WADA YOSHIMORI, MIURA YOSHIMURA, *and the rest—stand,
sit, or crouch. They are all dressed in rehearsal clothes. On
top of the various boxes scattered about are piled their costumes and a few properties.* WADA YOSHIMORI, *a man of
large build, with sideburns, stands up with a shake of his
head.)*

WADA: Well, shall we go ahead with it? Or perhaps change
it? Once again, from beginning to end? I must say, after
going through it once, I'm bored to tears.

*(MIURA YOSHIMURA, a stern-looking man with a melancholy face,
speaks half in self-derision).*

MIURA: Nothing to be done about it. I mean, look: he's got-
ten where he is. And the situation makes us impatient.
Well. I can't imagine how he can stay so cheerful, with
that happy expression on his face.

WADA *(coming closer to* MIURA*)*: Miura, you seem quite calm
about the whole business, I must say. But after all, what

[100]

good does it do to go on repeating and repeating something? The whole thing happened almost eight hundred
years ago. And we've finally been able to start giving up
all our mutual grudges. Isn't that right?

MIURA (*rising slowly*): As far as I'm concerned, the whole
thing irritates me. It's not that I feel any remorse over
what I did before. I'm not like you. I don't shrink from
work that turns out to be bloody. (*Stopping* WADA, *who
begins to say something.*) What I hate is to have to repeat
something once you've done with it. You remember: we
set out to do the whole thing in great earnest. We were
really angry. And full of resentment. With hate in the
pits of our stomachs we slaughtered each other. But if we
do it all again, the whole thing will just turn into a travesty of itself. Worthless. Oh, I agree that those who
witness all of this might find something of interest there.
But as far as I'm concerned, I'd somehow feel as though I
were making fun of myself.

WADA: What if we just give up on the whole thing?

MIURA: Now wait, it may not be so easy. Suppose Sanetomo
tells us to begin? What then? Refuse? Our relations with
him have never permitted that.

WADA: I still don't understand. The whole thing must have
been terribly painful for him. And this particular incident was the most painful of all. There's no reason to
repeat this needless torture. So why, now . . .

MIURA (*with increasing self-scorn*): What is there to understand? He's always been a complete mystery to me, ever
since this whole business began. If there is anyone who
does understand, point him out to me at once. I wonder.
Who was he really?

ŌE (*his hair sprinkled with white, speaking without expres-
sion*): Great Manor Lord of Japan, General Warden. The
Third Kamakura Shōgun. Chief Commander of the
Warriors. Lord Minamoto Sanetomo.

[101]

MIURA (*shaking his head*): Yes, I suppose that is how it sounds in the history books. And don't forget about how the court nobles might have seen it. Great Minister of the Right, with Senior Second Rank. Poet of the Empire, author of his own poetry collection.

MASAKO (*softly, but quite explicitly*): No. He was my son. Until the time of his death, he was devoted to me, a proper child to his mother. The Hōjō power lasted for one hundred and fifty years. And it really began with that child.

AZUSA (*in a somewhat abstracted fashion*): That gentleman was my husband. With him, the house of Minamoto finished forever. But my husband kept until the end his splendid lineage.

CHEN (*standing and looking at the rest*): You are all wrong. He was not merely your Shōgun. Not merely a poet. Not merely a Hōjō. Not merely a Minamoto. Not just a warrior. Not just a nobleman. All this is wrong. He is a saint in my country of China, and greatly honored.

KUGYŌ (*in a loud, irresponsible voice*): This is all a lot of nonsense. He was a murderer. Why, he killed his own brother. He was a filthy thief who stole the title of Shōgun. Dead, he is, and he has no business even sitting with the rest of us.

WADA (*walking closer to* YOSHITOKI): I'm sorry, but I just don't understand. Who was he? And what was he trying to become? And what was he plotting to do? Can't anyone tell me? I was the first one he made a display of, the first one who was murdered. I have a right to know.

MIURA (*as if to tease* WADA): Anyone will do. Because there was no "who" for him to be. He was clever enough to never truly reveal himself. Then again, it seems to me that we ourselves may have been taken in, seduced by shadows.

WADA (*approaching* YOSHITOKI): Lord Yoshitoki. You are certainly the one who should understand. You can tell me. Because you were really like a father to him.

YOSHITOKI (*after a short silence*): But I don't understand either. We've been trying to explain our feelings to each other for the eight hundred years since we descended to this place. What were we plotting? What were our reasons for doing what we did? He's the only one who has never so much as ventured a single word about the whole thing. In this, I'm just like the rest of you. All I do know is what he showed us then, on that platform, and at that time.

WADA: I just don't believe it. After all, at the time we were all alive you were the closest one to him, weren't you?

YOSHITOKI: I'm sure it seemed that way. And I was terribly fond of him. But for me too he was like some lovely nimble bird. Seduced by the glitter of those beautiful wings, and, notwithstanding my own shrewdness, I allowed myself to be taken in by his whole bearing, that manner that was so hard for me to grasp. And I began to meddle in things. I ran around, trying to put a rope on him, to pull him into my hand, so that I could observe him at leisure. It was all for nothing. As a result, I only succeeded in driving the poor boy into a corner and killing him.

WADA: Well, I suppose such an explanation can satisfy you. But what about me? I was killed for a man whose motives I don't understand. And I'll just go on, after this, even though I'm dead, understanding nothing.

(YOSHITOKI *rises without speaking. He then reaches into his robe and pulls out papers which might be a script, a scenario.* WADA *catches sight of them.*)

WADA: Say, what are you doing with that? Are you thinking to go ahead with it? Lord Yoshitoki, even you . . .

YOSHITOKI (*laughing*): When you remember something that happened to you in the past, something you still don't

understand, then what do you do? You act the whole
thing out again in your head. To see if there's any way
things might have turned out differently. But when you
use your whole being to recreate that moment, then
sometimes you suddenly remember some circumstances,
some complications, that you'd completely forgotten
about. Sometimes the body can remember things the
head has long ago rejected. Then, without thinking about
it at all, you can suddenly understand the meaning of
everything. Do you see? Come then, Wada Yoshimori,
don't make a face like that. In any case, Sanetomo has
asked us to go ahead. And perhaps this is the means he
has chosen to reply to all our suspicions. (YOSHITOKI *lifts
his right hand, and as he signals, the stage suddenly darkens.
To the accompaniment of faint music, the sky behind changes
to a strange red sunset.*)

Scene Two

VOICES: Sanetomo! Sanetomo! (*With this whispering as a background chorus, the voice of* YOSHITOKI *can be heard reading
aloud, in the midst of the darkness.*)
YOSHITOKI: 1213, early spring. This year, Sanetomo is twenty-
two years of age. His court rank is Senior Fifth Rank,
Lower Grade, Middle Captain, Inner Palace Guards, Division of the Right. He is the third Shōgun to rule in
Kamakura. Fourteen years ago, in 1199, Sanetomo's father, Yoritomo, died. This brave general, who founded
the Kamakura government and who ruled as the first
Shōgun, died after falling from a horse. But various
rumors about that incident have continued to circulate.
In 1204, Sanetomo's older brother Yoriie, the second
Shōgun, was murdered. To be quite straightforward
about it, I killed him. Actually, both of us did. I was
helped by my older sister Masako. She was his mother. I

was merely his uncle. We murdered him. Let there be no
misunderstanding there. The following year, we did battle with our father, Hōjō Tokimasa, in order to protect
Sanetomo from him. And our father gave in to us. That is
how, with Sanetomo, the title of Shōgun passed once
again to its legitimate holders, the Minamoto family.
Since that time, ten years have passed. And so quickly.

*(As the light above the platform changes to that of a realistic sun-
set,* WADA *and* MIURA *appear from stage right.* SANETOMO *plays
with his* kemari *ball sitting on the spar, but the two do not notice
him.* MIURA *looks at the crimson sky.)*

MIURA: Look. The sky is still that bewitching red. I can't help
but think it will bring a storm. Maybe even an earth-
quake.

WADA: Whatever happens won't be any surprise. The whole
world seems in turmoil. There's no reason why heaven or
earth alike should let this injustice pass unnoticed.

MIURA: Yes, I certainly appreciate how concerned you must
feel. Was it today that you visited your nephew, Lord
Tanenaga, in prison? Was he in good health?

WADA: I don't mind telling you that Tanenaga is a splendid
soldier. He is worried about me and about the future of
our family. I don't know how much torture he's had to
suffer. Even though I'm a high official myself, they're trying to find some clue that I too might have committed
some crime.

MIURA: It is inconceivable that the Shōgun himself could permit warriors to be put to torture. In any case, not a
member of the Wada family, that has rendered the
Shōgun's family such distinguished service.

WADA: No, of course it's not the Shōgun himself. What do
you think Lord Sanetomo knows? It's the work of that
Hōjō brother and sister, his uncle Yoshitoki and mother
Masako. I'm sure Sanetomo did understand one thing
though. That Tanenaga has been caught in a trap. He's
been accused of making plans for some kind of insurrec-

tion. There's no fool stupid enough to think that he had anything to gain by aiming an arrow against a Lord he clearly serves for loyalty.

MIURA (*laughing treacherously*): His loyalty was the cause of his misfortune. I'm sure you remember that. Before, all the clan of Hiki, whom Lord Yoriie designed to favor, were killed off by Sanetomo's uncle, Yoshitoki. And for the same reasons.

WADA (*suddenly raising his voice*): The situation is not the same at all. I attacked the Hiki clan myself. The motives of that bunch and of my nephew are entirely different.

MIURA (*taking a different tack and speaking in a flattering voice*): I daresay you are right. Nevertheless, Yoshitoki is in a constant state of apprehension. That Sanetomo might gain some powerful allies close at hand. In any case, as far as the Hōjō are concerned, the Wada family is quite dangerous at the moment. And precisely because they helped the first Shōgun, Yoritomo. Their great service has been to help establish his power in Kamakura.

WADA: Things were wonderful in the old days. There was only Lord Yoritomo in charge. There was a warm, living sense of understanding between leaders and soldiers alike. Once in a while the horsewhip came flying when he lost his temper. But on the other hand, there on the battlefield was the general of the whole army, dozing with my own shoulder for a pillow. But how do you think things are now? The warrior's court has become a place to argue out one's greed. It seems the faces of those pasty-looking officials have a tendency to come between a master and his men. Why, I myself haven't had a real audience with Sanetomo for more than two months.

MIURA: That's just the way Yoshitoki wants it. This seems to represent his so-called new method of government.

WADA: And that's just why the warrior spirit will wilt and die. Why, Miura, if it were a question of a rebellion, then

Sanetomo should go ahead and cut off my nephew Tanenaga's head himself. And if it were a question of Sanetomo himself—some mad act on his part—then we would
willingly accept. Everything. But now we have to sit
around and wait for some judgment to be handed down
by a court. Even though someone's neck is in danger, it
doesn't seem to matter any more if our master is angry or
sad. Everything is bound up in some infernal logic. The
plan seems to be to arrange a murder through some kind
of mutual consent.

MIURA (*a cold smile passing over his face*): I follow you exactly. If that's the case, then what do you intend to do
about it? I agree that something must be done to help
your nephew Tanenaga, but the Hōjō are very powerful
adversaries.

WADA: I hear that Sanetomo still holds Tanenaga in high
favor. I must somehow search him out, get down before
him, and beg him to grant some sort of special pardon.

MIURA: Do you think it can be done as easily as that? So far,
Sanetomo has never had an occasion to countermand
Yoshitoki's wishes. You mustn't forget that. And Yoshitoki's great influence is not simply because of Sanetomo.
Have you observed the young warriors these days? All
their memories of war have somehow faded. They seem
all too happy to enter into a world populated by peaceful
bureaucrats. Logic alone seems to get by all too well.
Battles over land get settled in court instead of on the
field. Everyone says that Yoshitoki's judgements are fair.
And among the young ones, at least, he has a pretty high
reputation.

WADA: Fair. They say his judgments are fair . . .

MIURA: That's what the younger ones are saying. In their
eyes, none of these disputes has any larger significance.
Each one of their heads is stuffed full of their own little
concerns about their own little plot of land. No wonder

Yoshitoki has become so popular, spreading his bait among a crew like that. "Fairness." Well! And thanks to all that, he has managed to lay a trap. Suddenly there's a conspiracy, and we're the offenders.

WADA: If that's how it is, what are we supposed to do then? Just what are you telling me that I should be doing?

MIURA: You and I have both been fighting Yoshitoki in the arena he has already picked out for us. There's no chance for us to win. The only possibility is for us to change the arena.

WADA: Change the arena? What does that mean?

MIURA: There is one thing you have more of than Yoshitoki. That is force. Power.

WADA (*looking* MIURA *full in the face*): Are you telling me . . . that I should start a rebellion? Start a war?

MIURA: Look here. There the Shōgun himself sits. This is a splendid opportunity. Why don't you throw yourself on his mercy, in the most open and honest way you can?

WADA (*frozen in fear for a moment, he then totters forward a few steps and falls forcefully on his knees*): My lord, I have found you at a most opportune moment. I, Wada Yoshimori, wish to petition for the most important request I have ever made in my life.

(SANETOMO, *with great agility, bounds down from the yardarm; with his back to the two of them, he keeps his eyes shut and does not move.*)

WADA (*raising his head*): My Lord.

(SANETOMO, *without answering, takes the ball that he had in his hand and throws it over his shoulder.* WADA, *without thinking, catches it with both hands, then turns round.*)

SANETOMO: So, Wada, you were the one. The one who caught it.

WADA: What, my Lord? The ball? What do you mean?

SANETOMO: I was trying out a bit of soothsaying. Children often do this sort of thing. You know, how to pick out one person in a group. The one that something is going to happen to.

WADA: But what kind of soothsaying were you trying to do? Do you mean that something will happen . . . ?

SANETOMO: Don't make so much of it. I always amuse myself by telling fortunes. Like reading the rings of trees, or pulling off grass stems for a lottery. And, because I do it so much, my luck suddenly changes. I suddenly feel as if all the pain, all the horrors are disappearing, and I have a vision, a bewitching vision of my own future fate. (*He pulls from his robes the stalk of a leafy plant.*) Look here now. For example, will Sanetomo drown tomorrow, when he swims in the sea? . . . Or not? . . . Drown? . . . Or not? (*As he says this, he pulls off one leaf after another.*) Drown . . . not . . . yes . . . no . . . yes. Well, well. It seems I'm going to drown tomorrow in the sea at Izu.

(WADA *and* MIURA *look at each other apprehensively.*)

SANETOMO (*bored*): Well then, try again. Drown . . . or not? Drown . . . or not? Yes . . . or no? Ah! This time I don't drown. That's about all you can expect from this sort of thing. But don't think that I regard all this fortune-telling as a lot of nonsense. My fate for tomorrow is swaying back and forth, even at this very instant. Right, left, right, left. Win, lose. Live, die . . . Then suddenly everything will stop. And no matter how many times I try, the same result will come up. And that means that I . . . that I . . . (*As he speaks,* SANETOMO'S *face hardens in fear. He drops the stalk in his hand.*)

WADA: My Lord. (*He edges forward on his knees.*) Please listen to me. I have a wish I earnestly beg you to grant. If you could only listen . . .

(*In an instant,* SANETOMO'S *expression softens. Quietly taking the ball from* WADA'S *hands, he turns around and, with a lighthearted gesture, kicks it into the air and catches it in his hands. He speaks in a gay voice.*)

SANETOMO: Miura. What do you think this is? This. This big post?

MIURA: Why, it looks to me more like the mast of a ship than anything else . . .

SANETOMO: Exactly. This is the mast for a ship in the Chinese style. There is nothing like it in Japan. A thousand-stone Chinese ship. Just recently someone sent me the plans and drawings up from the capital. This ship is not like the ones we build. It is supposed to move along continuously, even in a headwind. To build a ship just like this is a horrendous job. But with the mast up, at least the men can begin to learn how to handle the sails. (*He throws the ball to* MIURA *and lightly clambers back up the mast.*) What about it, Miura? There's a splendid view of the sea from here.

MIURA: My lord, are you thinking to have such a Chinese ship built right here, on this beach?

SANETOMO: I agree it looks difficult from the plans. And I wonder what my uncle and my mother might say.

MIURA (*laughing ironically*): I doubt that your mother will be very enthusiastic. After all, sailing around on ships can be quite a dangerous thing to do.

SANETOMO (*suddenly cold*): I should know my own mother. She isn't the kind of woman to have any fears as commonplace as those. If you don't believe me, why don't you go to my brother Yoriie's grave, poor murdered man. Go there and find out for yourselves. Find out if she's been weeping around there once, even once.

MIURA (*flinching; then, with irony*): I see. But then, after all, we're just talking about a ship. Isn't it just a plaything, just another form of make-believe for you to spend all that energy on?

SANETOMO: It doesn't matter what it is. No one thinks that what they are doing is just playing. Yes, isn't that precisely the point? War or politics, it doesn't matter. No wise man would go so far as to deny that perhaps everything we do is just playing, in great earnest.

MIURA: You are perfectly right. In that case, if you finish your ship, where do you intend to sail with it? To China? India? Or perhaps . . .

SANETOMO (*hopping down from the mast, he comes right up to* MIURA, *then takes back the ball*): You seem to have forgotten. I am the Shōgun. The Ruler of Kamakura. If I should simply sail off to India, what do you think would become of this country? Or, if I managed to vanish from the scene, would things be somehow more convenient for all of you?

MIURA: Why . . . why that is ridiculous!

SANETOMO (*bursting with laughter*): If the ship is ever finished, I shall send some brave lord off to India, I think. And when it comes to that I don't think there's any more suitable candidate that Miura Yoshimura himself. (*He throws the ball back to* MIURA, *who is most alarmed and throws it back and turns his face away unhappily.*)

WADA (*coming forward, he kneels down before* SANETOMO): I have a request to make of you. I beg you earnestly to consider me for such a duty. Since the days of your poor departed father, all of us in the Wada family have given up our whole lives to serve the Minamoto. I, and of course my nephew, Tanenaga, would happily go to the ends of the earth if need be to carry out your orders. But My Lord, because of a vile slander, the whole Wada family is now tossed about like a frail boat in the rapids. Please do not forget about us. Since you were a child, Tanenaga always served at your side. In the camps on freezing winter hunts he warmed your feet with his own body. When a fox was cornered and, in its suffering, tried to bite you, it was Tanenaga who dashed to shield

[111]

you with his own right arm. And now this very Tanenaga of whom we speak lies moaning in a prison cell.
And all this because some rumor of an insurrection has
reached Your Lordship's ears . . .

SANETOMO (*who has been listening with his back turned, suddenly, irritated, interrupts him*): The sky is red. An ugly
shade of red.

WADA: I beg you, listen to me. The judgment will surely be
made tomorrow. Whatever kind of cooked-up comedy it
may turn out to be. And Tanenaga . . .

SANETOMO: This is all very tedious. Tedious, and long-wind-
ed, Wada Yoshimori. (*A long silence.* SANETOMO *turns
around and looks intently into* WADA's *eyes, then averts his
glance once again.*) It is not necessary to go on and on
about all of this. Now that the situation has gone this far,
I am suddenly in a position to appreciate his affection for
me, his feelings of pain and suffering, and so on and on.
I know all of this. In fact, that's just the means he
thought to use to make his complaints about me. Despite
the fact of ten years and more of service, my feelings
toward him had always been deficient. And so on . . .

(WADA *is speechless; he looks up at* SANETOMO *as if someone had
struck him.*)

MIURA (*as though waiting to ask about something*): . . . He
thought to make use of all that to complain . . . If that's
the case, then you, Sanetomo, must feel it is true that
Tanenaga has somehow behaved in an improper
manner . . .

SANETOMO (*he turns around fiercely, sharply*): Miura, you
wouldn't understand. I am severe. Whether there is any
truth to that allegation I don't know, but I do know that
he has opposed the Hōjō family since the beginning. He
was fond of me, and so for my own sake he set himself in
opposition in every respect. All of this kind of thing
might be very interesting for you. For me it is hideous. I

will not bear it. (*Tears glisten in his eyes. Then he speaks again, softly.*) Wada Yoshimori. You are a cruel man. You want to force me to remember. Do you think I can forget? I must have been five years old when, held in your arms, I went on a visit to the great Hachiman Shrine. My father was in good health, and my older brother and sister were still well. When I saw my older brother and my mother chatting together so amiably, who would have ever guessed the gruesome ending? It was just when the spring leaves were opening. I remember the tickling of sunshine strong enough to burn my neck mixed with a crisp wind, teasing my cheeks. I was so happy. You were all there, and you were joking about something with my uncle Yoshitoki. I remember. You were laughing in a big voice.

(MIURA *and* WADA *stare at* SANETOMO; *they look as if they have swallowed their own breath. Suddenly* WADA *puts both of his hands to the ground.*)

WADA: Thank you, My Lord. Having seen these tears in your eyes, there is but one more thing I would like to say. If Your Lordship's feelings might be conveyed to Tanenaga in prison, then the whole Wada family will tell him of your benevolent judgment.

(WADA *weeps.* MIURA *stares doubtfully at* SANETOMO. *A pause. Suddenly* SANETOMO, *with a facetious gesture, faces the darkness at the bottom of the platform and throws the* kemari *ball. It seems as if someone catches it, then* HŌJŌ YOSHITOKI, *dressed in a kind of court robe, silently walks onto the platform.* MIURA *and* WADA *relax and pull themselves together. Then a number of young* WARRIORS *and* ARTISANS *hurry in from all directions and kneel on one knee.*)

SANETOMO (*turning, in a commanding manner*): You men are late in coming. The daylight is almost finished. While it is still light, the practice must begin as soon as possible. Rokurō, you go over there. Hachirō, go up there. Saburō, you climb the mast. Well, Uncle Yoshitoki, have you, too, come sightseeing today to look over the little toy navy?

YOSHITOKI (*greeting them all, lightly*): It looks like everyone is gathered together for exactly that same purpose. So that I can keep up with the times, perhaps I, too, can have the privilege of watching from a corner.

SANETOMO: Why of course. There's nothing I do that I wouldn't welcome you to take a look at. (*To his men.*) So then. We have lots of visitors today. Get your spirits up; be proud. So then. Begin.

(*The men disperse.*)

SANETOMO (*raising one hand*): Watch the wind.

ARTISAN (*calling out*): A fair wind.

SANETOMO: Check the tide.

ARTISAN: The tide too is good.

SANETOMO: Let out the sail lines.

ARTISAN: Aye, aye, Sir.

SANETOMO: Prepare the yard.

ARTISAN: Aye, aye, Sir.

SANETOMO: Prepare the anchor chain.

ARTISAN: Aye, aye, Sir.

SANETOMO: Take the sail lines. Pull!

ARTISANS (*sound together*): Ho . . .

SANETOMO: Pull!

ARTISANS: Ho . . .

SANETOMO: Pull!

ARTISANS: Ho . . .

(*The men, shouting together, pull on the ropes. With the sound of music the stage dims.*)

Scene Three

(*Below the platform falls a faint golden light by which* WADA *and* MIURA *can be seen looking at each other.* MIURA *pokes at* WADA'S *shoulder, as if to tease him.*)

[114]

MIURA: Somehow or other, I knew that you weren't keen on the whole thing. But you really did get up there and put all you had into it, didn't you?

WADA: Well then, and how about you? You're the one who kept saying how much you detest this sort of game, but you put yourself into it too.

MIURA: Curious, isn't it? As soon as you appear before him, you get swept up in his own animation. You laugh, you cry. You know it's only a play, but somehow everything suddenly seems to have turned real. I wonder why that's so . . . ?

WADA (*shaking his head*): I don't know. However you look at it, this doesn't really seem to be a play. Unless I have holes where my eyes should be, he's not the man to manufacture counterfeit emotions.

(*In a different corner beneath the platform,* KUGYŌ *is groaning.*)

KYGYŌ: Ha. It's his damnable charm. Once cheated and you still don't remember? His technique consists of cheap theatrics. His real feelings are nothing more than chips and splinters. And here's the proof of it. His face is like a dead man's. It shows no emotion at all. None at all.

(SANETOMO *descends the platform and his face can be seen in the direction in which* KUGYŌ *is pointing. It is motionless, as though he were wearing a* nō *mask. He is perfectly still, a tableau vivant.*)

Scene Four

In an instant the area below the platform darkens, and a bluish-white light, suggesting moonlight, falls on the platform above. The sails, ropes, etc., have all been cleared away. The area now seems to represent a garden.

MASAKO (*from below the platform*): This will never do, Yoshi-toki. Meeting Wada face to face, at a time like this. Whatever you may think, the dangers are too great. (*She *mounts the platform from stage left, followed by* YOSHITOKI *and* ŌE HIROMOTO.) And that child is by no means as strong in character as you seem to think. He may be tested in this manner any number of times. And at some point I wouldn't rule out the possibility that he might come to feel like betraying us.

YOSHITOKI: In Wada's case, I wasn't thinking of any test at all. Masako. That boy is the Shōgun, the Ruler. Anyone who wants to can meet him; my only duty is to see that he's not tied down. That's all.

MASAKO: The Ruler? I am the Ruler, Yoshitoki.

YOSHITOKI: I realize that full well. You are always the one who makes the final decisions. And of course no one is allowed to forget that you have already sacrificed one son, Yoriie. How noble of you. My dear sister, a Shōgun needs to make decisions, but a Shōgun also needs wisdom. And more than anything, he needs a face that manifests both.

MASAKO: Of course. You have the wisdom, and he has the handsome face. That's fine, don't you think? But wisdom tends to weaken a person, and anyone with a beautiful face gets lost in dreams of how to show himself off. That is the danger. Here's what I heard from someone who was there: Sanetomo took kindly to the appeal that Wada made to him and seems to feel satisfied with the whole business.

YOSHITOKI: That's nothing but some busybody bearing tales. I saw the whole thing with my own eyes. Everything is fine. He didn't say even a word, not one word, to give Wada Yoshimori any reason for encouragement. There was no hint of any agreement.

MASAKO: But he cried, didn't he? Or maybe, to put on a show of fairness, this was a play put on for your education.

YOSHITOKI: Ridiculous. What is the purpose of such a play? They were real tears, I'm sure. After all, he is a true

Minamoto, whatever you might say. He is different from us. He really is quite fond of an old-fashioned, sincere retainer like Wada Yoshimori.

MASAKO: And that's precisely what is so dangerous. That was just the problem with Yoriie. He adored those old-style warriors who took so much pride in their brute strength. It was the burden of having these people around that finally forced him to begin his opposition to us.

YOSHITOKI: Don't worry. Sanetomo is not like Yoriie. He knows something about the problems of using power. He's no youngster in that sense. In the arena of politics, there's no worry that he'd set himself up against us.

MASAKO: I must say I'm surprised by you. You really are fond of that child! I'm his mother. And how many times have you defended him to me?

YOSHITOKI: I know, I know. But actually, sometimes I can't help responding to the simple honest feelings of a young man like that.

MASAKO: What a charming story. But then, who do you think will believe it? The only thing you really like is putting the whole country under your thumb. And hasn't the boy been a useful marionette to help you accomplish precisely that?

YOSHITOKI: What a terrible thing to say. My dear sister, you have misunderstood me completely. I don't really know what to tell you at this point. Suffice to say that I did want to have an opportunity to try out my own way of thinking. And could such a way of thinking serve as a means to govern or not?—I wanted to test my own intelligence too, in order to find out. You of all people should have understood this. In any case, it certainly never occurred to me that I should take your place and put the whole country under my domination.

MASAKO: I see. Apparently what you say may have some truth to it. Now that I think about it, you are an unusual

[117]

man. When you can merely test your intelligence, you are completely satisfied. But it seems you never know what you want to obtain by using that intelligence.

YOSHITOKI: On that point you are pretty remarkable yourself—I don't know anyone who is so clear about what she wants as you. That's the very reason we make such a good combination.

MASAKO: In any case, it all comes to the same thing. The boy is a puppet for you to use to practice your intelligence on. But it seems to me altogether excessive when that puppet begins to feel, think, and worst of all, shed tears, all by himself.

YOSHITOKI: I see you think you have the whole thing figured out. Shall I go on? In order for someone to manipulate another like a puppet, he must first grasp the real feelings of that person. He must make him feel, make him think as though he were free. And when his mind and heart have been seized altogether, the victim will feel at ease. Then he can be manipulated. But if that boy is tied down and restrained in any clumsy fashion, he will decide to hide his real feelings. That, I can assure you, would be terrible.

MASAKO: Exactly. If so, I wonder why there is any need to do anything that is simply bound to get him all excited. In any case he is much too susceptible to things as it is. He'll sit weeping over the wind blowing at the end of the porch. Or he'll see the waves breaking over the shore, say he's fascinated, and waste practically half his time staring at them. It's all very well when he can make a poem out of all that. But then the poems make the boy's feelings that much stronger. He's becoming positively infatuated, it seems to me.

YOSHITOKI: Come, come. Nothing to worry about. As long as a man is moved by poetry, there's no danger at all. People's real passions are seldom aroused when they're all

[118]

absorbed in choosing some clever little word or appropriately discordant harmony.

MASAKO: I'm not joking. These days, Sanetomo is seeing strange things. Isn't that so, Hiromoto? Last month, for example, I heard he saw a weird light, and that he loitered around all night in the palace garden.

ŌE (*lowering his voice to indicate his seriousness*): Yes, this occurred once two months ago, and twice last month. And the strange thing is that his Lordship seems to have had it in mind to meet a ghost. Recently, these nocturnal walks have occurred time after time.

MASAKO: I heard that he's not in his room tonight. Yoshitoki, there is absolutely no reason to get this child more excited than he already is. Things have to be made quite clear to him. For his own sake. Who he is. Who his enemies are. Who his friends are. If he's not considering the importance of these pending questions in his life, then it's no wonder, with the weakness he has, that he's taken to seeing ghosts, or whatever. Tonight we must find him and explain to him just what kind of judgment has to be handed down to Tanenaga. Without fail. (*She hurries off the platform at stage left.*)

YOSHITOKI (*to ŌE, in an ironic tone*): Well, well. There doesn't seem to be any shortage of ghosts in Kamakura at the moment. There is Yoriie. Then there's the rebel general, Kajiwara Kagetoki, and all the Hiki family too. How strange this all is. What has Sanetomo done to provoke them? If anyone should be seeing ghosts, it's certainly me.

ŌE: No, My Lord. It may be you who first bent the branch, but it is Sanetomo who now tastes that delicious fruit.

YOSHITOKI: To all those in my generation who are dead, what a scoundrel I must seem to have become. Things always turn out this way. Men understand so little of each other's real intentions until they get to the other world.

[119]

ŌE: And what of Lord Sanetomo? He's the one who really counts. I am sure that you understand each other so well . . .

YOSHITOKI (*after a brief silence*): I really don't know. And, up until now, I have never forced him to take any particular decision. When some political problem arises, I take it on myself. The opportunity has never really arisen for him to worry and make the decisions without me. So we've never had any occasion to really be angry with each other. But what does he believe, at the bottom of his heart? I haven't any idea. Does he really trust me? . . . I've protected him, fought for him. Or does he keep his doubts? After all, I killed his older brother.

ŌE (*nodding assent*): I see. Yoshitoki, now I believe I understand. You have decided at this time, in the case of Wada, that to test Sanetomo's real feelings . . .

YOSHITOKI: You mean you think the whole thing is a deliberate plot? (*His laugh is melancholy.*) You see, no matter what, I seem to come out the scoundrel. Well, that's all right too. But this time, the boy will make his choice for himself. That much is certain.

ŌE (*lowering his voice still further*): Please be careful, My Lord, for the ghost Sanetomo recognizes and wants so much to meet is real. But whose ghost is it? Could it be his older brother Minamoto Yoriie? Then, there is the persistent rumor that it is really his father, Yoritomo.

YOSHITOKI: Well, well, I see you have long ears, as usual. In any case, this is good news for me.

Scene Five

Soft music; points of light begin to well up in the dark sky. On closer inspection, the myriad bits of light look like flowers, perhaps butterflies.

VOICES (*whispering in a chorus*): Sanetomo . . . Sanetomo . . .

Sanetomo, Act One, scene two. Wada (David Liebowitz).
1976 Washington University production.

Sanetomo, Act One, scene two. Left, Miura (Dan Schaffey),
right, Sanetomo (Chao-ping Wu).
1976 Washington University production.

Sanetomo, Act One, scene two. Left, Sanetomo (Chao-ping Wu), right, Miura (Dan Schaffey).
1976 Washington University production.

Sanetomo, Act One, scene two. Sanetomo (Hosokawa Toshiyuki) and the sailors. 1973 Tokyo production.

Sanetomo, Act One, scene seven. Left, Azusa (Kaga Mariko), right, Sanetomo (Hosokawa Toshiyuki).
1973 Tokyo production.

Sanetomo, Act One, scene ten. Left to right, Masako (Sasaki Sumie), Wada Yoshimori (Kanai Dai), Azusa (Kaga Mariko), Sanetomo (Hosokawa Toshiyuki), and a warrior. 1973 Tokyo production.

Courtesy of Osamu Honda

Sanetomo, Act One, scene ten. From left to right, Yoshitoki
(Trip Bates), Masako (Barbara Schaps), Sanetomo (Chao-ping Wu),
Wada (David Liebowitz), Miura (Dan Schaffey), Chen (Stephen Pasternack).
1976 Washington University production.

Courtesy of Osamu Honda

Sanetomo, Act Two, scene six. Left, Kugyō (David Edelman),
right, Miura (Dan Schaffey).
1976 Washington University production.

(*Several seconds later,* SANETOMO *dashes onto the platform.*)

SANETOMO: Come. Appear. Show me your face. It's Sanetomo. I'm here.

(*The music seems to grow louder. From the gloom comes a shadowy* FIGURE, *dressed in pale robes.*)

SANETOMO: So. You were here. Who are you? What do you want to say to me? Well, open your mouth. (*He comes forward and kneels before the* FIGURE.) Please tell me. What is it you want me to do? (*The* FIGURE *suddenly fades into the gloom by the pillar.*) Wait! Why won't you say anything to me? (*He walks once around the pillar and rushes off the platform as if chasing the* FIGURE. *The bright light and the music fade. Only the pale sky remains.*)

Scene Six

(KUGYŌ *comes up from below the platform.*)

KUGYŌ (*shouting*): I can't stand it. Your methods are just too lenient. Why won't you pin Sanetomo down by the neck and force a commitment out of him?

(KUGYŌ *and* MIURA *mount the platform from stage right.*)

KUGYŌ: Lord Miura. Things are not working out at all the way they should. If you leave a situation to someone like Wada Yoshimori, everything important will get washed away in Sanetomo's crocodile tears. Your arguments are thoroughly logical. You've got to attack with them. You've got to drive him into a corner he can't get out of.

MIURA: Now just a minute, Kugyō. There's no point in cornering him for the moment. The really important thing is to drive a wedge between him and the whole Hōjō family.

KUGYŌ: And I'm telling you, with the methods you're using, that whole plan looks pretty doubtful. And what on earth is Sanetomo anyway? Is he really a willing tool of the Hōjō? Or is he a loyal member of the Minamoto clan like

[121]

me? He's got to be confronted directly and asked—which one is he going to choose?

MIURA: Am I the one who is supposed to tell him that? Making it perfectly clear that I set myself up as an enemy of the Hōjō family? That's no joke. The moment a man like me makes a statement like that, fighting will break out in Kamakura. I know that much.

KUGYŌ: Well then, what do you suggest be done? At some point or other I intend to attack my father's enemies. Do you mean to tell me to stand there with my arms folded, waiting for a break between Sanetomo and the Hōjō to occur all by itself?

MIURA: Exactly. And that's why I've told you what I have. Kugyō, you are the one. You're the very best choice. Meet him, talk to him. After all, you have ties of blood, you're his nephew. Meet him, just by yourself. Tell him straight out that you want to know what can be done for the Minamoto. For the moment, that means Tanenaga must be pardoned. If that happens, Sanetomo will be smashing down Yoshitoki's reputation with his own hand. But most important of all, don't give away your own real feelings. You've got to push him towards rebellion from his own initiative. Talk little, listen most of the time. See if you can work things around so that he speaks up against Yoshitoki of his own accord. Hint to him that he has the support of Wada Yoshimori and me. And let him think that he has support more powerful than that of Yoshitoki's. And, let me repeat again, keep your own desires to yourself. Whatever else happens, you must say nothing about the position of Shōgun. If the Hōjō rule is put down, you'll be next in line. After all, you have Yoriie's blood in your veins, and even if you don't say a thing, you'll have what you want.

KUGYŌ: Let me try then. I'll see if I can get him to speak freely. I must admit, when I see someone like Sanetomo, who goes right through life without the courage to get involved himself, it irritates me.

MIURA: Come now! When it comes to something as important as this, I think you can forget about your irritation.

KUGYŌ: On the contrary. It's not just that he stole the power from me. But why doesn't he even seem pleased about it? He must know all the resentment I feel. But why does he never reveal any fear of me? Looking at that cool face of his, you would think that wielding the Shōgun's power is nothing. Just nothing at all.

MIURA: Yes, but is it that he's crafty and merely hides his intentions? Or is he just a puppet, a Shōgun with no real feelings? You'd better know which is the case.

KUGYŌ: You're missing the point. He's trying to make a fool of me. He's making a fool of everyone, everyone who is at all in earnest. Let me explain. Any man, it doesn't matter who, carries around with him something that moves him, urges him on. It might be a grudge. It might be ambition. Or even something simple and touching, like wanting to eat until his belly is full. But he must have it.

MIURA: Very nice. Just the qualities that you have, I see.

KUGYŌ: You're laughing at me. And he's laughing too. But it's true. I want to be the Shōgun. I want to clear away the wrong done to my father. I want to seize the power of this country with my own hands. That is the man I am. And you know I'm that kind of man. And that's why you can trust me. You can deal with me. You can make use of me. But what about him? Just because he had a little bit of luck, he can laugh with scorn at a man like me.

MIURA: Well, that's all right, isn't it? After all, what's important for you is to take over the power. Whatever he may be feeling inside himself hardly matters, after all.

KUGYŌ: You really don't understand. I just can't bear this any longer. I could take solace in an enemy that took himself

[123]

seriously. But someone who makes a joke of his own earnestness . . . I couldn't support such a person, even if he were on my side. (*He leaves the stage.*)

MIURA (*watching him go*): What a dreary fellow. And a weakling. He wants to kill, but has to depend on the help of anger and hate to get himself up to doing it.

Scene Seven

The same night. Outdoors, but there is a small campfire burning, suggesting perhaps the corner of a garden.

(SANETOMO *and* AZUSA *stand, drawn close together.*)

SANETOMO: Why, Azusa. I can't read on your face what you may be feeling. Is the night wind too penetrating? Or does the darkness of this garden make you feel apprehensive?

AZUSA: No, I'm fine. Really. But I was just thinking it's been three years, three years since I came from the court in Kyoto and set my heart on learning how to make myself into the proper bride for a warrior. So I should be stronger by now than any girl brought up here in the first place.

SANETOMO: Exactly. You've become a splendid wife to the Shōgun. My uncle and my mother are both delighted. But still, I can't read that face of yours. Are you tired? You should go back to your rooms and rest.

AZUSA: Yes, I will. But I wonder. Why are you so observant of such small details? That may lead you to miss something else far more important.

SANETOMO: Something far more important . . . what could that be?

AZUSA: Something I can't quite explain, but it has to do with the surprising way you conduct yourself. You are always so gentle with me. You always tell me how beautifully I keep myself, how well I dress. But for more important things, no matter what I do, you seem to look on indifferently.

SANETOMO: Well then . . . can you give me an example?

AZUSA: For three years I've done everything I could to become the wife a warrior needs. And you tell me your uncle and your mother are pleased. But what about you? You haven't said a word.

SANETOMO: I love you. And whatever you are, that's fine with me. I love you just that way.

AZUSA: If we were two other people, in some other place, how happy any woman would be to hear those words. But when I hear those words from you they have a different echo to them. Is this the way it really feels when you're fond of someone? I feel as though I were wrapped in a warm cloud, infinitely yielding. Truly, I feel the need of something much, much more rigid, stricter.

SANETOMO (*suddenly joking*): I'm perfectly content. I adore your eyes. And I love those wise, sweet ideas you have. I love to hold you, my arms around your warm little waist. (*He draws her to him and strokes her lovingly.*)

AZUSA (*having entrusted herself to him in this fashion for a certain time, suddenly speaks in a resolute tone*): I'm going to ask you something terrible. We've been together all this time but we've never had a child. There is no successor for the Minamoto line. Why is it that you never say anything of this to me?

SANETOMO: We're young. There's plenty of time to think of children.

AZUSA: You don't think about the implications. If you produce an heir, there are many who will embrace their own wicked dreams for this country. That treacherous Kugyō; or Wada, Miura and the other warriors. Or your mother and your uncle may have similar thoughts with the Hōjō family in mind. What worries me most is this apparent

[125]

lack of concern they've manufactured. Anyone who has fearful expectations will act as though nothing were wrong, no matter how anxious he may be inside. On the surface they are gentle; they say nothing, but from the expressions in their eyes, they curse and kill our child who is not even born . . .

SANETOMO: You mustn't worry. Even without children, there is so much we can do while we're alive, so much that can bring us pleasure.

AZUSA: But what do you plan to do? You should have become the real ruler of this country. You write poetry. You build a boat. You seem happy and you seem busy. But isn't all this because, actually, there is nothing that you truly have to do?

SANETOMO: I don't see this as any joke. I certainly don't spare myself when it comes to my duties as Shōgun. I preside at the trials, and I put my seal on all official documents prepared. And I go to visit the shrines and temples once a month, to bring good fortune to my warriors.

AZUSA: I know all that. You're altogether diligent, and you enjoy all the work you do. But you do it too smoothly. You never quarrel with anyone, or push anyone aside.

SANETOMO: What nonsense! Such behavior is not necessary.

AZUSA: No, it would be necessary. If you had a child. If there was another like you who might go hungry, you would have to grasp your power tight, in both your hands.

SANETOMO: So you are as hungry for power as that, are you? I never realized the daughter of a court nobleman would be like this.

AZUSA: Not for my own sake. If it were all right with you, I wouldn't care at all what happened to the country. But if that were the case, I'd expect you to have some other dream. If you tell me you want to throw everything away to write poetry and wander about in some far away place, I would understand, and be pleased.

SANETOMO: How surprising. If I did something like that, what would become of you?

AZUSA: What if you told me to become a nun? "Suffer for the sake of Sanetomo," something of that sort. It might be painful but at least there would be a place for me in the world.

(*A short silence.*)

SANETOMO: Did you know that, before, I had another woman with me?

AZUSA: Yes I know. I don't know why she went off and left you, but I begin to understand her feelings.

SANETOMO: She was a person of no consequence, but I would have given anything up for her, anything, everything. The title of Shōgun, the Minamoto family, all the elegant poetry, all the artistic accomplishments. I'd happily have thrown it all away. And I thought she'd be delighted. Then one day, without so much as a word, she vanished. I suppose you understand. What could have gone wrong?

AZUSA: Of course. She loved that man. That man Minamoto Sanetomo. From a great clan—the Shōgun. You were a man who could truly build a life from all the things you liked and did. She adored all of this. And then you stopped becoming that person. And so easily.

SANETOMO: But it was all because of her. That's why I was willing to abandon myself.

AZUSA: Perhaps you are right. An ordinary woman would have been delighted. But I certainly can understand her. For you really don't love and respect yourself. (AZUSA *turns away fiercely and begins to leave the platform.*)

SANETOMO: Azusa. Wait. I . . . (*As* SANETOMO *hurries to follow her, the music starts up and the yellow sparkling lights begin to glitter again.*)

VOICES: Sanetomo . . . Sanetomo . . .

SANETOMO (*looking into the sky*): So you're there again . . . Where are you . . . ? Show me your face . . . I want to tell you something. I want you to do something for me. (*Searching out the* FIGURE, *he returns to the platform.*) Speak. I have the force. And strength of will. And too much curiosity. I'll do anything, try anything. Revenge an enemy? But who is the enemy? Risk some adventure? But where should I go? Speak. Tell me. Am I to live? To die? And what judgment am I to hand down tomorrow?

VOICES: Sanetomo . . . Sanetomo . . .

SANETOMO (*sinking down at the foot of the mast*): That phantom certainly has a high opinion of himself. If that is the attitude he's going to take, then I intend to wait him out. Well, well. What can I do? Come to think of it, perhaps you have nothing to say after all. (*He gives a great yawn.*)

VOICES: Sanetomo . . . Sanetomo . . .

(*The whispering slowly fades away;* SANETOMO's *chin drops and he falls asleep.*)

Scene Eight

(MIURA *mounts the platform from the left.*)

MIURA: This is all very strange, Yoshitoki. We have no summons to go up there and witness something like that last scene. There's nobody but him up here anyway. Do you really think something might have appeared? Certainly none of us saw anything at all.

YOSHITOKI (*with some care*): Well let's not make a fuss about it. And in any case, it's only a rumor that a ghost appeared to him.

WADA (*also discontented*): Why does he want to show us that last scene anyway? Does Sanetomo mean to say that it was the ghost and not he himself who brought all these misfortunes on us? I certainly don't feel like putting up with any idea like that!

YOSHITOKI: What nonsense. In the first place, the boy told me he didn't even meet the ghost. Well, let's watch. Af-

terwards everybody will know about it. In any case, Sanetomo seems shattered in a thousand pieces.

Scene Nine

(SANETOMO *is asleep on the platform. From stage left* MASAKO *quietly mounts the platform, with a sliding gait.*)

MASAKO: Sanetomo. Are you asleep? It is me. Masako. Your mother. I have something I'd like to speak with you about.

(KUGYŌ *enters from stage right, in the same manner.*)

KUGYŌ: Listen to me, Uncle. I've come, and I really want to hear what you may be dreaming.

(SANETOMO, *sandwiched between them, is still asleep.* MASAKO *begins to speak.*)

MASAKO: Don't worry, Sanetomo. As long as I am here, nothing untoward will occur in Kamakura. Look for yourself. Tonight too, everything is calm and quiet. In the last seven or eight years, there are fewer and fewer warriors who spend their nights quarreling. Even the partisans of the Emperor, watching our every move from Kyoto, have no pretext over which they can take advantage of us. They too have lost their desire to fight. Sanetomo, there is nothing to worry over. Nothing to think about. Our administration moves forward, like a sail filling in the wind.

KUGYŌ (*shaking his head furiously*): Uncle, there is one thing you must never forget. No matter how good your politics, you cannot build on the hatred of the victims you have sacrificed. Listen carefully. Amid that night wind that seems so calm, you can hear the sobbing of all those noble men who have been ensnared by the Hōjō. Uncle, you now sit in the seat you stole from them.

MASAKO: Never forget what happened to your brother Yoriie. What happened to that poor child was worse for me, his mother, than for anyone else. Still, what else could have been expected? He loved to dress up and parade around the streets, but he didn't really have the patience to listen to the demands of his warriors and hand out honest judgments.

KUGYŌ: Land disputes, water disputes. Any woman can solve those problems. Turn them over to subordinates. A great and powerful Shōgun should have more manly work to occupy his time than that. Bureaucracy can take a man who, on his horse, could rule the country, and try to bury him alive in a mountain of documents and account books.

MASAKO: The Shōgun for these times is not for the battlefield. In times of peace, people tend to be jealous of a strong leader. Rather than a leader, they welcome a busybody. For a person to really govern a generation like this one he would have to retire from active life.

KUGYŌ: What a clever, evil scheme. And because of it, the whole country has lost any sense of purpose and has fallen asleep over its fatuous desires for the future. Listen, Uncle. A wise ruler must place himself boldly between his friends and his enemies. If someone is jealous, give him reason to be jealous. Whatever happens, they're not the ones who have to be consoled and satisfied anyway. As for the weak ones, they can be overturned by strength. And they'll finally come around to accepting their bad luck by themselves.

MASAKO: You must never be taken in. And in any case, it's not a question of one man moving the world these days. It's a question of a kind of common-sense logic that anyone can understand, and of planning out a government run on that kind of common sense.

KUGYŌ: Logic may appeal to people's heads, but it's not going to move any hearts. Anyone who wants to get the world moving today won't do it with some little plan.

[130]

He'll be a violent man. It's still not too late, Uncle. When your father was murdered, you were just twelve. It wasn't in your heart, but you became the Shōgun anyway. I suppose you, too, were sacrificed, just like the rest of us. But from now on, things will be different. Tomorrow, at the trial, if you sell off the whole Wada family to the Hōjō, at that point you will truly have stolen the role of Shōgun from your older brother.

MASAKO: Just remember this. When you were fourteen, your grandfather, my father, Hōjō Tokimasa, was determined to keep you from becoming the Shōgun. My brother Yoshitoki and I, forgetting our own feelings, found it necessary to use force against our own father. We felt that no one, not even our father, had the right to usurp the power for himself. And that the principles of government must not be bent out of shape for the sake of a family. Now that old man, condemned in the very trial you presided over, lives out his own sad life, exiled to live deep in the mountains of Izu. Sanetomo. Do you mistrust my sincerity? Or that of Yoshitoki? The same political logic dictated the murder of your brother Yoriie. Your ascension to Shōgun is part of that same necessity. If you try to rebel, you will become guilty of stealing the power not only from your brother Yoriie, but from all those who have been defeated by that logic.

KUGYŌ: Choose then, Uncle. For the first time in your life, make a choice yourself.

MASAKO: This is a lot of foolishness, Sanetomo. For ten years you have followed that logic. You have been a fine Shōgun. And for ten years, making those distinctions, you yourself have made the choice to be the person you have become.

(SANETOMO *suddenly lifts his head and looks around him.* MASAKO *and* KUGYŌ *seem to disappear from sight as they slowly stand and begin to move one or two steps away. The music and the yellow lights vanish.* KUGYŌ *and* MASAKO *draw backwards and leave the platform. Replacing them is* YOSHITOKI, *who mounts the platform.*)

YOSHITOKI: Well, well, what's all this about? A poetic turn of mind is all very well, but rumors of an all-night vigil by the Lord of Kamakura, in a place like this . . . ! There are those, unfortunately, who would rejoice to hear about it.

SANETOMO (*without turning around*): Ah. My Uncle Yoshitoki! Are you out for a walk as well? I was looking here for some orchid plants. These are the first this year. There was a whole bunch of them blooming here until night-fall. But when the moon came out, I lost sight of them, mingled in the moonbeams.

YOSHITOKI: If these orchids interest you, go back and look in your own rooms. I had some cut and arranged there for you. I remember your poem about the blossoms of bush clover:
"Bush-clover flowers bloomed
until the verge of night;
When I went back to see them,
in the moonlight,
they had vanished:
Impermanence."

(SANETOMO *is silent momentarily. Then he speaks cooly, without irony and with a touch of resignation.*)

SANETOMO: Uncle, when I want something, you seem to know more about it than I do myself. You always antici-pate me, and you always manage to grant me more than I wished for.

(YOSHITOKI *is also silent for a moment. Then he laughs, in a deso-late fashion.*)

YOSHITOKI: In fact I think you're right. I can. And if I could manage to do it without your being aware of it, then I would be a first class guardian for you. Ah well. My training isn't yet sufficient for that.

SANETOMO: Thanks to you, I have no need to desire anything at all. Let me try that . . . ! Let me try this! I have no reason to agitate myself with thoughts like that.

YOSHITOKI: I suppose that aspect of things must seem a little tedious to you. Why not go off to Kyoto for a nice long visit—two or three years perhaps—and amuse yourself?

SANETOMO: Is this a declaration of war, Uncle?

YOSHITOKI: You amaze me. You have been studying politics a bit too assiduously. There is absolutely no need for it. It is certainly true that the present Emperor has detested this government in Kamakura, but there are not enough men available for him to think of raising an army. At this moment Kyoto and Kamakura are at the height of their struggle to obtain the loyalties of all the warriors in the country. I myself have confidence in the outcome. For if we can win that victory, there will be no more need for the throne to rise up against us as a rival. Do you agree?

SANETOMO: I hear that a messenger from the Emperor has been to visit Tanenaga during his confinement.

YOSHITOKI: Ah, so you hear about that sort of thing, do you? The Emperor has a strong arm indeed, and he seems now to have the idea he can thrust it into my very vitals.

SANETOMO: He knows of my feelings for Tanenaga and hopes to break apart the relationship you and I share together.

YOSHITOKI (*staring for an instant at* SANETOMO): So, you have understood things that far. And if you have, then will you listen to something more? I would like to tell you, to the best of my ability, the real truth concerning this current incident.

SANETOMO (*extremely quietly*): No. No, Uncle. Things are fine as they are. There is no need for it.

YOSHITOKI (*letting out a light sigh*): I suppose that's how you see it. You really don't want to hear about it. Tanenaga was a fine soldier. And so, so I understand. In your heart of hearts you still don't trust me. That's not unreason-

[133]

able. Even if you hear an explanation from my own lips, your own judgment will be that much more confused.

SANETOMO: There is no confusion. I am the Shōgun. And whatever the Shōgun is to do, his uncle will explain to him, quite clearly.

YOSHITOKI: That's all right. There's nothing to be ashamed about over a little confusion. And making a judgment, even based on confusion, helps to root confidence in a person. I see what's happened, even though you don't tell me a thing. What have you spent a sleepless night up here worrying about? I suppose it's rude of me to say it, but I've been watching over you with the hopeful thought that you might be worried about something.

SANETOMO (*a low laugh, artlessly*): When an incident like this arises, everyone begins to say all sorts of things, don't they? Words, words, words. There are really no limits to what people feel they have to say.

YOSHITOKI: For a long time you have merely listened to my advice in silence. And now, because of the ache in your heart, you scrutinize my every word. You are trapped between reason and a gentle heart. You search my words for error and you hope to find a way to reject them.

SANETOMO: I have no anxiety. A man who has no choice of his own has no reason to feel any anxiety.

YOSHITOKI: As far as I'm concerned, I'm delighted to see you suffer. Because it means that, finally, you, along with me, have begun to think over the political situation in this country. And . . . well, that's enough, I suppose. You've surely suffered enough. Tomorrow, you must hand down a verdict and acquit Tanenaga.

SANETOMO: Acquit Tanenaga . . . but . . . why should I . . . ?

YOSHITOKI: For your own sake. The Emperor in Kyoto must already have learned that we in Kamakura are no fools. We shall give Tanenaga another occasion to drive the lesson home. Later, if you have a change of heart, that will be fine too. Because if this error of Tanenaga's is repeated, then you can satisfy yourself by having him punished.

SANETOMO: But Uncle, aren't you convinced? Without looking any further, there's no mistake. An offense has been committed . . .

YOSHITOKI: Just as I told you before, if it is necessary, I can show you the proofs. But . . .

SANETOMO (*rising, quietly*): Well then, there's no problem. Let us curtail all the tiresome procedures.

YOSHITOKI: But wait! Sanetomo! You . . .

SANETOMO (*suddenly resolute*): Well then, give me your report. As usual.

(YOSHITOKI, *his spirits put down, takes out the document, which has been folded over, and hands it to* SANETOMO, *who takes it and lifts his hand high in the air. From the gloom sounds the crash of a staff violently striking the floor.*)

Scene Ten

(*As the stage fills with light, all the characters hurry quickly to their places.* SANETOMO *is in the center;* MASAKO, WADA YOSHIMORI, MIURA, AZUSA, *and* KUGYŌ *are arranged in a semicircle.* WADA TANENAGA *is standing in front of them. He never speaks. Behind them jostle the* WARRIORS *with flags and weapons in their hands. There is a kind of curtained tent behind them. One* WARRIOR *pounds the floor with a staff.*)

WARRIOR: Lord Wada Tanenaga. Judgment concerning you will be handed down at these proceedings.

(SANETOMO, *holding a written record of the decision, steps to the forward part of the platform.*)

SANETOMO: Wada Tanenaga. You have conspired together with dissident elements from the court in Kyoto in an attempt to overthrow our Shōgunate. From the proof we

have seen this fact is abundantly clear. Such a crime cannot be overlooked by Heaven, and certain death is its
price. Nevertheless, long years of fidelity cannot be overlooked. Therefore I sentence you to banishment in the far
province of Mutsu. Your lands and domains will all be
confiscated. Now, until further notice, you will be
handed into the custody of Wada Yoshimori. (*As* SANE-
TOMO *finishes reading his proclamation in a disinterested
manner, he turns his back to the audience and enters the
tent.*)

WADA (*screaming as he rushes to the center of the stage*): Wait!
Wait! Is this the judgment? I don't understand. Lord Sanetomo when . . . when did you change your mind? (*Several* WARRIORS *apprehend* WADA.) This is hideous. Were
all those tears completely false? Or did someone, in the
space of one night, manage to change that man's mind?
Whatever happened, the outcome is clear.

(*The stage lights suddenly darken, leaving the light on* WADA,
who crouches down on the floor.)

WADA: Lord Sanetomo. Now my own hopes, and the hopes
of all my family have been extinguished. Why not take a
sword to my head, and let me finish a laughing-stock. In
what way should a faithful warrior die?

(*As* WADA *rises, a voice screams out of the darkness; at the same
time the stage is flooded with stark white light, which goes off and
on. The banners have fallen, the tent has collapsed, and all those
on stage rush off the platform with grievous cries. In the midst of
all this, three or four large wooden horses appear on the platform,
and as if they were in a chase, begin slowly to circle the mast,
borne up by the* WARRIORS. *The sounds of shouting and battle
noises continue;* YOSHITOKI *comes to the edge of the platform.*)

YOSHITOKI: We are now in the fifth month of the year. Wada
Yoshimori, leading his whole family in a party of one
hundred and fifty men, swooped down on the Shōgun's
mansion at Okura. The Shōgun's own dwellings were
burned and the whole Wada family fought as though

they were demons incarnate. But the rebellion was suppressed in a day and a night. This is because Miura Yoshimura, who had promised Wada his support, betrayed him and gave his allegiance to the Hōjō.

(The screaming voices reach their highest pitch, then begin to fade, the flashing lights die out, and the stage falls quiet. Low music begins, and a soft light falls.)

Scene Eleven

On the platform two of the fallen wooden horses are piled on each other, as if to suggest the remains of a terrible battle. The stage is littered with flags, tent curtains, and various military accoutrements.

(At one side, SANETOMO sits astride the only horse left standing. In one hand he holds WADA's costume, as he looks over the confusion of the scene. Dim light falls beyond the platform as well; WADA, who has lowered his head, now lifts it and begins to mumble to himself.)

WADA: I just don't believe it. However you look at it, those were not false tears. They were not. Every time I think about it again, I know that his eyes showed love and sympathy. But if that's so, then Sanetomo is just a weakling. Yes, he's weak-spirited and he can't acknowledge his own true feelings. I must resign myself.

MASAKO *(self-importantly, inspecting the surroundings)*: Just look around. He evidently listened to what I told him. Really, he's still only a child. Of course, he shows a considerable sensibility, but he has no real craving to live in this world. If things aren't explained to him, he won't even remember what his own feelings are.

KUGYŌ *(in a low moan)*: He's finally shown his true character. A hypocrite wise in his victory. But remember this. You've stained your hands this time. So from now on, it won't be enough to deal with me in any gentlemanly fashion.

Sanetomo

MIURA (*slowly shaking his head.*): Be careful. It's not just a question of a wise hypocrite. He's a young man who likes to play with people's feelings the way he might tear off the wings of dragonflies or butterflies. He's the kind who would enjoy feeding a chicken before wringing its neck: he is foolish enough to take pleasure in the poor bird's false hopes. As a tyrant, he shows genius. He is the kind of adversary who can give great wounds. And in the most thoughtless manner.

AZUSA (*trying to express the emotion in her voice*): He has thrown away something again this time. Something inside him, something terribly important.

ŌE (*whispering in* YOSHITOKI's *ear*): Anyway, there's nothing to worry about. After all, Sanetomo's decision shows that he's really taken the logic of Yoshitoki's politics to heart.

YOSHITOKI (*heaving a sigh as he rises*): I wonder. Is that what you call a decision? I don't know. That amounts to saying something pretty disagreeable about me.

(SANETOMO, *on top of the platform, gets gently down from the wooden horse, sees a shield that has fallen over, and reverently places* WADA's *costume on it, as though he were offering up a silent tribute to his remains. Then, several seconds later,* SANETOMO *mounts his horse again, and turning, he speaks in a light-hearted voice.*)

SANETOMO: The traitor has been destroyed. To celebrate our victory, let us go to the great Hachiman shrine, to offer our prayers.

(*With shouts of joy the* WARRIORS *rush onto the platform. The wooden horses accompany them on either side.*)

Curtain

Act Two

The stage arrangements are the same as in Act I. The costumes and props used have been left at the base of the platform. If a curtain is not used, the actors who play the WARRIORS *can arrange the stage in view of the audience.*

Scene One

The lights come up. Strong lightning; the sky in the rear swirls with strangely shaped clouds; thunder rolls out over the sound of driving rain.
(*Two* SAMURAI *run across the stage.*)

SAMURAI 1 (*out of breath*): What about it then? Will the eastern embankments hold, or not?

SAMURAI 2 (*also breathing heavily*): Who can tell? With a rain like this, another half day and trouble will start. What about the south walls?

SAMURAI 1: A while ago the upper bridge broke loose. The broken beams were washed down against the lower bridge, and now the water is rising there. If that pile of timbers doesn't get broken up, there is a good chance the water will overflow the banks.

(*Several* SAMURAI *hurry by, carrying hoes, straw bags, etc.*)

SAMURAI 1 (*after giving them instructions*): What a terrible thing. This rain has gone on for ten days now. We never see the real sky at all any more.

SAMURAI 2: It's supposed to be summer, but the sky is just like the ones during the rainy season. Everyone says there's some kind of curse. And I'm beginning to feel that way myself.

Sanetomo

SAMURAI 1: It's true. Ever since what happened, there has been no letup. One natural disaster in Kamakura after another. Earthquakes. Tidal waves. And a blizzard in April. Not a drop of water in the rainy season, and now this terrible downpour.

SAMURAI 2: When you say "what happened," do you mean what happened with the Wada family? That doesn't seem to explain anything. It's been three years now since all that business. No. That's not what the Hōjō retainers say now. No, they talk about a curse of Hōjō Tokimasa. When he died last year, at Izu. After he was exiled by his son Yoshitoki and his daughter Masako.

SAMURAI 1: Ah. That means the Shōgun is involved. Sanetomo. There are getting to be too many ghosts in Kamakura. And every one of them is unhappy about a different thing. Their curses show it. Which ones should Sanetomo take into consideration when he makes his plans? Now there's a tough one for you.

SAMURAI 2: Slow down a minute. There have been some changes. Since the Wada family was destroyed, Sanetomo has changed. He seems to have new energy. Everyone says so. He takes an interest in rendering his court judgments. He goes on with his official duties. Never misses a day. This morning for example. He said he would offer prayers to the Dragon God. And he stayed there, all day long, in this driving rain.

SAMURAI 1: What! Is His Lordship still there? He's been there since the day before yesterday.

SAMURAI 2: Yes, out on the nose of that cliff. The rain falls and the spray from the waves splashes over him, but he never moves at all. He doesn't eat, he doesn't drink. He sits there praying, his body bound fast to a log.

SAMURAI 1: That's all so surprising. I too heard that Sanetomo had changed, but . . . to that point. . .

SAMURAI 2: It really seems as though a curse has fallen on the curse! He's changed that much. Look around. Among the young retainers, some carry earth for the embankments, and they have tears in their eyes.

SAMURAI 1: We'd better be off. Before we realized it, we seem to have become the retainers of a brilliant leader. And if a rain like this destroys the embankments, right in front of that brilliant leader, the reprimands will be something terrible.

SAMURAI 2: You're right. Besides, if we don't provide some encouragement, we won't be able to face those youngsters who work under us.

(*The two step down from the platform and leave the stage; as they leave,* MIURA, KUGYŌ, *and* CHEN HO-CH'ING *enter.*)

CHEN (*to* MIURA): So. What do you think? It is as I said, no? Sanetomo is a saint. A holy man. He is the Healing Buddha. Born again. He prays for us. At the risk of his life. The power of the Miraculous Law. The rain of your Japanese gods is nothing in comparison.

MIURA: Well. I suppose that's another way of saying that he's praying. But Chen, the rain has to stop sometime, doesn't it? I mean, even if things go well, that's no reason to say that it was his praying that did it.

CHEN: Yes, you are right. Rain stops by itself. That is Heaven's Providence. But . . . what of the embankment? When rain comes, it always soon collapses. Now, days have passed; it does not collapse. Well. The farmers, the warriors are working hard. But, why? Because all can see him. Praying to the Dragon Gods. You Japanese, your wisdom is insufficient. In my country, such strength is called the strength of a saint.

KUGYŌ (*pulling at* MIURA's *sleeve and whispering*): Look, look— that's why I told you what I did. You mustn't underrate Sanetomo. These past years, he's managed to hold the loyalty of his retainers with just this kind of trick.

MIURA: I still don't see the point. It certainly does seem like someone has gone and put some sort of curse on things.

[141]

But this force has been disrupted. Because just when it seems the warriors are going to be deeply affected, Sanetomo turns around and uses some trumped-up excuse to amaze them all over again. (*Taunting* CHEN *in his turn.*) Now, Chen. All this business about the ship. How is it coming along? I hear that Sanetomo's real intention is to construct a ship large enough to sail off to China. Is that so?

CHEN: His real intention? What shall I say? I already have drawn plans for him. He is learning the words of my language from me. He goes to the mountains himself. To choose the lumber himself. He waits now only for permission from his uncle, Yoshitoki.

MIURA: Well, but what is all this about? Sanetomo has always been fond of ships, but he never said he wanted to sail off to another country. Because, in point of fact, he is the ruler of *this* country.

CHEN: No. You are wrong. This Lord is a lord of respect in my country. When he understood this, his feelings were set. For, indeed, anyone would wish to see his true country.

MIURA (*his mouth close to* KUGYŌ's *ear*): Now listen to this. Maybe Sanetomo is trying to flee the country. And he's put a lot of energy into it. But just what is he really up to? The situation still needs some looking into.

KUGYŌ (*closing in on* CHEN): Now, Chen. Let us have the real truth. For precisely what reason are you filling his ears with this "Buddha Born Again" story? After all, you were called by the court to carry out some repairs to the Great Buddha at Nara. What kind of plot got you all the way up here to Kamakura?

CHEN: No so. Not so. I filled his ears with nothing. I only said: he is like a senior disciple of the Healing Buddha. I only said it seemed *like* a rebirth. And then you, Sir, saw it yourself. His body swayed. It shook. And as was said before. He so spoke. What I said: the story is true. That he knew it from long before. Because of a dream.

[142]

KUGYŌ: So at that point, you pulled out your plan and got him all excited about it. I see. What did you do it for? Are you getting a reward? Or is the whole thing just a means to get you home?

CHEN: Not so. Not so. I believe deeply. One sees him, one understands. The more one sees, the more one respects. This is not a lie. In Japan or in China, I, Chen Ho-Ch'ing, will never leave his side. (CHEN, *thinking to escape, steps down from the platform.*)

KUGYŌ (*poking* MIURA *in the chest*): Now I see the whole thing. The entire ridiculous story—it's Sanetomo who created it and has been filling *him* up with it. I don't yet quite see the point. But in any case, it must have something to do with winning the people over to his side. Some kind of plot like that. Miura, it's fine to proceed prudently. But if we don't take action soon, our enemies will be all that much stronger.

MIURA: But I'm still not certain. If all this is so, then why go to China? A voyage by ship is terribly dangerous. And even if the trip is successful, Sanetomo would be out of Japan for more than two years.

KUGYŌ: True enough if you believe the story. But there is another purpose to that ship. He'll try to attack us. And if he fails, he probably thinks he can sail to the capital. Or even further, to the south . . . Well, so much for that. Let's go and see what we can find out. What kind of play is he putting on, with that pious face of his, for all those trusting warriors . . . ?

Scene Two

(*During the darkness, the sound of fierce wind and rain. As a dim light finally spreads onto the platform,* SANETOMO, *his body tied to the mast, stands up, lashed by wind and rain.*)

VOICES: Sanetomo . . . Sanetomo . . . (*The whispering now seems to come from far away, as if carried by the wind.*)

[143]

SANETOMO: What's happened? Why does your voice seem so far away? What is it that you want of me today? I'm sure you would never tell me to make a fool of myself the way I'm doing right now. Well, I agree with you. But if this sort of thing doesn't please you, then be specific. Tell me exactly what I should be doing. Ha! What about that? You don't know what to say, do you? From now on I'll make things just as difficult for you as I can. Because until you tell me something, I'll have to go on doing things in whatever haphazard fashion I can manage.

(*The* VOICES *fade to inaudibility.*)

SANETOMO: So then. You are running away, are you? (*He lets out a loud laugh.*)

(*The stage darkens.*)

Scene Three

(*The sound of the wind and rain is faint in the distance.* MASAKO, YOSHITOKI, *and* ŌE *enter.*)

MASAKO: I am absolutely against it. It will not do to force things along in that fashion. The child has always been infatuated; now he thinks he's divinely inspired. For all we know, he might turn into a real hero.

YOSHITOKI: On the other hand, you can't really be dissatisfied. After all, the boy has played the role of Shōgun in just the way we designed it. And if there isn't a bit of the hero involved in that role, then the people have nothing to set their own hearts on fire.

MASAKO: Well, well, since when have you become such a turbulent politician? Who was it that told me over and over again that the whole point of politics was to lower the national temperature? Wasn't the key to your new technique always negotiations over war? Haven't you always urged gluttony and idle chatter over pride?

[144]

YOSHITOKI. Of course, the people must be quieted down. But not to the point of boredom. Along with peace of mind, they need a certain amount of harmless indignation. We must provide enough stimulation to provoke lively discussions over the supper table. Look at it from that point of view then. How about it? Our young Shōgun in prayer, beaten on by the rain. I thought it would make the beginning of a kind of pious anecdote. Exactly what we need at this time. The only thing I'm really worried about is that he might catch cold.

MASAKO: Your idea in itself is perfectly fine. But you can't impose it on the child. He is so susceptible to suggestion. You think it's all a play. But what if he gets to the point of turning the play into the real thing? Then what will you do? Even if you use the excuse of the financial accounts and his meddling in people's affairs. You won't find him so simple to get rid of as we did his brother Yoriie. And let me tell you, I don't have time to give birth to another Shōgun for you!

YOSHITOKI: Of course you're right. Actually, I have been somewhat worried myself, on a slightly different point. You see, Sanetomo has been showing far too much loyalty to me. In fact, by playing the role of Shōgun so faithfully, and to my design, Sanetomo means to secretly rebuke me. As you well know, over-fidelity is one kind of opposition.

MASAKO: That's exactly what I'm telling you. You must not go too far. And you must find a way to divert his attention to other things. For example, let him build that toy he's craving for.

YOSHITOKI: The Chinaman's ship? I certainly don't think much of all that. I don't really understand his motives there. And if he has any real longings for China, we're really in danger. If a Shōgun feels a loyalty to any country but this one, the peril is real.

[145]

MASAKO: You always blow your worries up too much. After all, he's my own child. How could he love any spot in the world except the one where his own dear mother lives?

YOSHITOKI (*laughing softly*): On the other hand, consider this. We have always thought of him as a child of the Hōjō family. But actually, he may well consider himself a Minamoto. And, born a leader of the warriors, he still has the reputation of sharing the tastes and attitudes of the nobility. His heart has already been divided in two. I hesitate to state flatly that he hasn't started to look on China as his spiritual home.

MASAKO: Yoshitoki, you are carrying your joke a bit too far. After all, you've explained the whole thing yourself already, haven't you? As you said, the child is over-faithful to your commands.

YOSHITOKI: Yes, and it is the very fact of his fidelity that worries me. If a person really throws himself into a human relationship, some disagreement, some quarrel is bound to arise from time to time. He more than meets my expectations when I ask something of him. I have no idea what his true feelings might be.

ŌE (*rubbing his hands together, as if to put a word in edgewise*): I must admit that on this point I feel some concern as well. I speak of Sanetomo's rapid rise at court. Recent instructions from the capital have been most unusual, it seems to me. His ascendency is altogether untoward. In the sixth month of this year he was appointed a Provisional Middle Counsellor. Only a month later he was raised to the rank of Middle Captain of the Palace Guards, Left Division. Despite all of this, Sanetomo is still evidently unsatisfied. Recently he has sent a messenger to the court with a request that he be raised to the rank of Middle Counsellor. What can all this mean? After all, Lord Sanetomo is barely twenty-five. His rank will have risen three grades in one year. I must admit that all of this gives me a most uncomfortable feeling.

YOSHITOKI: Look carefully at the situation, Masako. The boy's allegiance seems to have gone over to Kyoto. If he should make the mistake of becoming the Great Minister, he will be a Commander-in-Chief with the military as his enemy.

MASAKO (*raising her voice, she laughs*): I just can't imagine why those who count themselves as that child's allies are borrowing trouble to this extent. Are the understandings of kindred souls so fragile as all that? Don't worry. Playing with boats, wanting to be toy minister—let him do what pleases him. If he really loses his head, his mother will take steps to put things right.

YOSHITOKI (*lightly letting out a sigh*): And what an amazing mother you are. You seem completely prepared to prevent your child from growing up.

MASAKO: When my husband died, I was determined not to live to grow old. I cannot, for the sake of the country, permit any proof that I *am* growing old.

(YOSHITOKI *and* ŌE *look at each other.*)

WARRIOR'S VOICE (*from below the platform*): Look! The rain has stopped!

ANOTHER WARRIOR'S VOICE: It's clearing up!

(*The rain has stopped and the sky clears.*)

ŌE (*in amazement*): The rain has stopped. Yes! It's really stopping.

(*The clamor of fierce voices. A number of* WARRIORS *push their way onto the platform as if to embrace* SANETOMO.)

WARRIORS' VOICES: Hurray! Hurray for the Shōgun!

(*As the voices continue,* MIURA, KUGYŌ, CHEN, *then* AZUSA *appear and surround* SANETOMO. *The clouds begin to break up, and the sunlight creates a kind of halo around the haggard figure of* SANETOMO. *The stage suddenly becomes quiet as* CHEN *hurries forth in a gesture of worship.*)

CHEN: Gratitude, gratitude to you, O Great Elder. We are not worthy. Indeed you have rescued us. Miraculous. Miraculous Living Buddha. We are not worthy of you.

[147]

Sanetomo

(SANETOMO'S *body suddenly begins to tremble violently*.)

SANETOMO (*in a voice not his own, as though in a delirium*): Let us go home. Yes, Chen Ho-ch'ing. Let us go home. To the west. To China.

(*He collapses*. AZUSA *supports him. Everyone is in an uproar*.)

AZUSA: Sanetomo! Oh, Sanetomo!

(MASAKO *screams, and* SANETOMO *slowly lifts his head; then an instant later, he springs up lightheartedly, as if nothing had happened*.)

SANETOMO: Uncle. I thought the whole thing over. All night. In the rain. I've decided that I should go ahead and have the ship built. I realize that consultation with the Supreme Council is necessary, but I want to hurry the project along as soon as possible. I have decided to do just what I want to do. Just this once. And Uncle, I'd like you to agree to it with a good grace.

(YOSHITOKI *looks intently at* SANETOMO. MASAKO *comes forward*.)

MASAKO: No, Sanetomo. It is fine to build the ship, but your attitude cannot be permitted. You may be the Shōgun, but you still must follow the regulations of the Supreme Council. Those are the rules of this new Kamakura. You of all people should understand very well.

SANETOMO (*gently, showing his disappointment*): Is that so? It isn't possible? Never mind then. Let me ask something else of you. Actually, Uncle, I did think that . . .

YOSHITOKI (*with unexpected force*): No, you are the Shōgun. If you want to do something, go ahead and do it. As for the Supreme Council, I myself will make any arrangement necessary.

MASAKO: But Yoshitoki! You . . .

(MASAKO *forgets what she wants to say. Once again* YOSHITOKI *and* SANETOMO *observe each other closely*.)

SANETOMO (*after a brief moment, brightly*): Uncle, I am grateful for your kind words. Well, then, everyone, from tomor-

[148]

row on we're going to put all our energy into the preparations. But before that, let us all feast! All I've had is
rain water, and my stomach is empty! (*Laughing loudly,
he begins to exit.*) And, oh yes, Uncle, it seems I will soon
be appointed as Middle Counsellor. The information is
confidential. Day before yesterday, a communication
came from the court at Kyoto. Now everyone, let us put
all formality aside!

(*Abruptly taking* AZUSA'S *arm, he hurries off the platform. The*
WARRIORS *follow him, raising loud voices in congratulation.* MASA-
KO, YOSHITOKI, MIURA, KUGYŌ, *and* CHEN *remain standing,
each showing the complexity of their feelings as the lights dim
quickly.*)

Scene Four

*From the darkness, mixed with the sound of hammers, chisels, and
saws, comes the sound of men as they bustle about.*

(*As the stage brightens,* WARRIORS *on the platform carry lumber
and hammers. Among them stand* SANETOMO *and* CHEN, *giving
instructions.*)

CHEN: Saburō! Don't cut the teeth on the cog so fine. Look at
the plan, follow it. Hachirō! Insects have eaten this
board. Do you see? Hurry, change it for another. Otherwise, what will resist the waves when they come at us?

(*A yellow light falls below the platform.* YOSHITOKI *stands up.
The bustle and noise fade slightly; actions on the platform are performed in pantomime.*)

YOSHITOKI (*reading aloud*): 1216. On the twenty-third day of
the eleventh month of this year, Sanetomo was elevated
to the rank of Middle Counsellor. On the following day,
Chen Ho-ch'ing, maker of Buddhist images at the Tōdai-
ji temple in Nara, was officially commanded to build
a ship capable of sailing to China.

WADA (*impatiently rising*): Just what is all this, Lord Yoshitoki? You're turning him into a person whose motives

make no sense to me at all. Since Sanetomo killed me, he's really gone crazy. Is that it? Or, if he is in his right mind, he certainly amuses himself at our expense. I'm coming to the conclusion that it is perfectly foolish to go along with this whole business any longer.

YOSHITOKI (*smiling forlornly*): If you, who are dead and looking on cannot understand, then do you think that those of us who are alive, and involved, can do as well? In any case, there is no way we can stop now. After all, we're the ones who are responsible for the whole thing in the first place. Not him.

KUGYŌ (*circling about in an irritated fashion*): It is all very boring. Why go through all of this just so we can understand him? Disgusting, that's the only word for it. All you are doing is giving him the opportunity to play one of his great dramatic scenes.

(YOSHITOKI *silently lifts his right hand, and the sound of work resumes on the platform.*)

CHEN (*showing exaggerated surprise at* SANETOMO'S *instructions*): This is . . . this is your real intention? The ship is now a ship of one thousand stone. If you make it double, two thousand stone, all plans must be redrawn. I have never myself seen such a ship.

SANETOMO: You have no confidence in yourself then? To tell you the truth, I have none in myself either. But let's give it a try. The Shōgun of Japan goes to pay his respects to the Emperor of China. I ought to be allowed at least that much adventure.

(CHEN, *hesitating, hangs his head.*)

SANETOMO (*aware of* CHEN'S *attitude*): What's wrong, Chen? Have you lost your courage?

CHEN (*faltering*): I . . . truly . . . truly . . . I . . .

SANETOMO: What's bothering you? Tell me, go on.

(*As* SANETOMO *puts his hand on* CHEN'S *shoulder,* CHEN *suddenly throws himself prostrate on the ground.*)

[150]

CHEN. Forgive me, Sanetomo, forgive me. I am a liar. I have
lied. Everything, everything is a lie.

SANETOMO (*after a moment's pause, with a loud laugh*): The
whole thing was a lie then. That I am reincarnation of the
Great Healer? All of that? Well, don't worry, Chen. I
knew all about that.

CHEN: You knew. But if you knew . . .

SANETOMO: Of course. And I have told some lies too. That I
had a message in a dream. All that sort of thing. But it's
fascinating to say those things. Don't you agree? Don't
worry about it. Because it *was* all quite fascinating, Chen.
(SANETOMO *laughs loudly. The noise of the work grows
louder again. The stage darkens.*)

Scene Five

(*As the lights come up, a large umbrella has been opened and
placed on the stage. Under it sit* YOSHITOKI *and* MASAKO. ŌE *and
one or two other* WARRIORS *stand in attendance. Before them pass
some* ACROBATS *who perform a few tricks.*)

YOSHITOKI (*looking intently at* MASAKO): What's wrong? Are
you worried about something? Here we are on this outing on a glorious fall day, and you still look positively
gloomy.

MASAKO: It's because I don't have any idea what you're up to.
Why on earth do you insist on teaching that pliant, obe-
dient child to rebel? He has started building his boat
with a frenzy calculated to make me nervous. You know
it as well as I do.

YOSHITOKI (*laughing lightly, full of self-confidence*): The boy is
putting up all the opposition he could ever be capable of.
That's not very much. As soon as I saw him, I knew everything was all right. He looks just as gay and bright as
ever. He shows the same diligence now that he has
always shown in his legal judgments, in his administra-

[151]

tion, and in his pilgrimages. There's nothing at all to worry about. There is no falsehood written on that cheerful face.

MASAKO: I don't see what you're driving at. Why does all that make you so pleased? I don't care whether his expression is honest or false. I don't care what he's feeling, so long as he steers the administration along in proper fashion.

YOSHITOKI: I see. But a false countenance could betray us.

MASAKO: Nonsense! That's just why we were determined to use logic and to establish efficient political methods. A man bound by logic and methods will hardly set out to turn traitor.

YOSHITOKI (*after a short silence*): I think you feel the same thing about me.

MASAKO: It's not like you to make a remark like that. After all, a man who gets himself into politics has no reason to voice those kind of feelings. Politics uses force to move men's bodies and create their destinies. It's a lucky thing we have inherited the requisite strength. Counting on a man's inner convictions is pure luxury.

YOSHITOKI: I agree. You're perfectly right. But don't you think I can be allowed one pleasure? I have no interest in debauchery, and the idea of stacking up treasure doesn't appeal to me at all. What a curious temperament. I can move the world around at will, but when all is said and done, there is nothing left in my hands that I can say is mine.

MASAKO: You really are a strange person. Why, you can have absolutely anything you want.

YOSHITOKI: But, you see, there is nothing that attracts me. Now take the Emperor in Kyoto. You know him. He may be my foe, but I have to say that he has the true ruler's temperament. He adores women. He piles up treasure. He snatches one huge estate after another from his subordinates and makes them his own. He wants to put the whole world in motion and he covets every piece of land he lays his eyes on. And despite the fact that he already knows that, as a sovereign, his name will go down in history, he's still not satisfied. He writes poetry and he assembles anthologies. He wants to give his name to a great sword blade and even plays at being blacksmith. He's made the chrysanthemum his symbol and amuses himself by carving the flower all over his palaces. I must admit all that seems strange to me. But I must envy a man who feels he can give concrete shape to a symbol of his own existence like that. He seems a man who has really lived. He has seen the logical workings of the world and he can live in that world, satisfied, and on those terms.

MASAKO: How odd to hear you speak like this . . . From what you say, I realize you want the boy. You want to make his very feelings your own. Isn't that right?

YOSHITOKI (*after a short silence*): In the end I suppose one man is not born into this world in order to have any real encounter with another. Although nothing could be more useless, more transitory than knowing the man you meet, there is a kind of luxury in pursuing this. A luxury that is hard to abandon.

MASAKO: If you start talking luxury, no logic can stop you. What will become of all this? If the boy fawns on you, how far will he go to contradict you?

YOSHITOKI: Don't worry about that part. The boy has a good head. And he has a better grasp of my political ideas than I do myself.

MASAKO: Well let's hope things are as they appear to be. But when that ship is finally finished, what's going to happen? Will the child really sail it off to China? Or won't he? That's when the two of you will begin your own battles.

(YOSHITOKI *assumes a stern expression.* SANETOMO *rushes on stage.*)

SANETOMO: Mother, excuse me for having kept you waiting. Actually, it's because I met up with *this* on my way.

(AZUSA *enters carrying an* INFANT.)

SANETOMO: Look at this poor baby. It's been abandoned. The poor thing is exhausted. It can't even summon the energy to cry. Its parents must be poor, but even so their behavior is hard to forgive. Apes in the mountains behave with more propriety. If an offspring dies, the parent will remain until the body mummifies. (SANETOMO's *voice suddenly clouds over and he cannot speak.*)

MASAKO (*gently*): These unfortunate children. It may be the floods, but I hear that the number of children abandoned in Kamakura has greatly increased. What do you plan to do with this one?

SANETOMO: To begin with, I'm going to issue a decree tomorrow forbidding the practice of abandoning children. I've also decided to use this opportunity to have Azusa open a proper orphanage. I've already found a suitable temple for the site. And I'll pay for the project with my own personal funds.

MASAKO: (*lightly ironical*): Such a lovely gesture. As Shōgun, you have found still another means to make all the farmers rejoice.

SANETOMO (*in a sudden change of mood, brightly*): Concerning this, Mother, I do have one request to make.

MASAKO: What might that be?

SANETOMO: May I ask you again to hold a proper memorial service for my dead brother? I would like the ceremony to serve as a model of parental affection to all these imprudent parents.

(MASAKO *is suddenly strained; her face hardens.*)

ŌE (*uneasily*): But My Lord . . . That . . .

(SANETOMO *and* MASAKO *look at each other intently. After a silence,* MASAKO *laughs coldly.*)

MASAKO: Of course. What you suggest is perfectly reasonable. I will call all the priests in Kamakura together and

plan the service. Tomorrow. And I would like to give
some help to Azusa and the orphanage. Don't fret, Ōe.
You should be delighted. As you can see, Kamakura has
seen three generations of great rulers. Now I think I will
retire for the day. So many happy things have been accomplished. I feel my outing is at an end. (*She gets up
from her seat with determination.*)

SANETOMO (*saluting her vivaciously, in a rather joking manner*): Thank you, Mother. And I think these services will
serve your purposes as well. And Uncle, there's also
something I want to talk over with you. While looking at
that poor orphan, I suddenly thought of our Kugyō. He's
already seventeen. He'll soon have to begin thinking
about his future.

YOSHITOKI (*who has been listening to all of this with interest,
arms folded*): Well, well. Have you any wisdom to share
on the subject?

SANETOMO: Why not appoint him the steward of our Hachiman shrine? It would be quite appropriate—to serve the
clan God of our Minamoto family and to carry out proper
duties in honor of my dead brother.

YOSHITOKI: Well! I must say that's an unexpected means to
deal with the problem. However, I think for work of this
importance, he's just a bit too young.

MASAKO (*interrupting, sharply*): You need say no more, Yoshitoki. After all, he is speaking now as the Shōgun. We
should carry out his wishes to the letter. I'm leaving
now. And Lord Ōe, I have some things to discuss with
you. I will expect a visit from you later in my apartments.

(MASAKO *turns and leaves the stage.* ŌE *and the attending* WAR-
RIORS *clear away the umbrella and the camp stools, receive the*
INFANT *from* AZUSA, *and follow* MASAKO.)

SANETOMO (*with an expansive gesture*): Thank you, Mother.
(*He turns round to* YOSHITOKI.) Uncle, this has been a day
of great ripenings. It's a rare thing when an outing like
this can produce such an unexpected harvest. Now I
must hurry off. The construction of the ship is now in a

most difficult stage. I want to build it twice the normal
size, but Chen Ho-ch'ing has turned coward and won't
give his consent. So I must excuse myself. There are
some things I'd like to talk with you about, but I'll have
to put them off until the next time I see you. (*He taps*
YOSHITOKI *lightly on the shoulder and, in a cheerful mood,
leaves the stage.* YOSHITOKI *and* AZUSA, *left behind, look at
each other.*)

AZUSA (*uneasily*): Uncle, are things all right left this way?

YOSHITOKI: Are you concerned about something?

AZUSA: Sanetomo's mother certainly seemed offended when
she left. She must have felt Sanetomo was giving her a
rude rebuke. And it's not difficult to see why. I was quite
taken aback myself.

YOSHTOKI: She may be my sister, but she cuts quite a figure
in her own right. She would never be cross because of a
mere slip of the tongue.

AZUSA: Well then, Uncle, how do you feel about what happened? You don't think that Sanetomo was showing
some real spirit of rebellion?

YOSHITOKI (*laughing, in good spirits*): I am absolutely delighted
by what he said. Just as Masako indicated, Kamakura
now has a third great Shōgun. It's not a spirit of rebellion
at all, but a sign of his ardor for politics.

AZUSA: Do you really think so?

YOSHITOKI: Perhaps you weren't quite aware of the situation.
Even if you look at what Sanetomo said as a political
strategem, it was an extremely shrewdly conceived
suggestion. Think for a moment. It has been fourteen
years since the assassination of Yoriie. People in Kamakura have begun to forget all those wild rumors that used
to circulate. So now, when Yorrie's own mother gives a
grand memorial service in his honor, all those who still
waver will have their last doubts removed. And for the
Shōgun himself to find an abandoned child at the same

[156]

time! As a story to spread around it's a creation of genius, I assure you. When we heard that marvellous plan, there was no reason at all for us to get upset.

AZUSA: I suppose you're right. That is, if he regards you and his mother as real allies. But should he think of you as enemies, then wouldn't you find his attitude today imprudent?

YOSHITOKI: What are you trying to tell me? Do you think that, in his heart, he does not believe in us, trust us?

AZUSA: I cannot tell. Even to me, Sanetomo never opens his heart. Still, I am sure what you have said is true. That he believes both of you, without reservation.

YOSHITOKI: Hm. (*He looks at* AZUSA.)

AZUSA: Yet think about the situation. It wouldn't be surprising if he had thought of rebelling, in his heart of hearts.

YOSHITOKI: I don't quite follow what you want to tell me. His trust in me is surely a friendly act on his part . . . or, on the contrary . . .

AZUSA: No, I don't mean that either. Just the opposite. If he is thinking to oppose you, Sanetomo is being very careless. I mean he's not being serious enough.

YOSHITOKI: Not serious enough . . .

AZUSA: That's right. If he wants to manipulate his enemies, you and Lady Masako are the most powerful adversaries he could have. His spoiled child attitude would be of no use. And he would need to think up some more clever, prudent plan.

YOSHITOKI: Exactly. So don't you see, that's why we don't think he regards us as his enemy.

AZUSA: If that's the case, why fine. But if you're right, why is he building that ship with so much determination? His mother is certainly not happy about it. And you yourself don't seem very satisfied by his explanations.

YOSHITOKI: That boy has great strengths stored up in him. And there is so much that interests him. There is nothing

[157]

to worry about. Look at the Emperor in Kyoto. He gets excited about far more foolish things than Sanetomo does.

AZUSA: But the Emperor really knows what he wants to do. Seize power. Make himself more important than anybody. Whatever he does, the Emperor keeps his attention on that one point. Always.

YOSHITOKI (*with a long sigh*): You have rather a sharp way about you.

AZUSA: But as far as Sanetomo is concerned, what is it that he really wants to do? You know, he has really become a different person. Before, he would waver over the slightest decision. Now he throws himself into any project with glee and vigor. Yet I feel unfortunately both attitudes are merely the same, underneath. First he seems to be working on the ship as though it were the most important project in the whole world; then suddenly he throws himself into arranging Kugyō's future. He prays in the rain and he decides to establish an orphanage. I don't feel that he's really sincere. He seems to find it all just a bit too amusing. Perhaps I am just overanxious. But sometimes, it seems to me that Sanetomo regards living as, well, as a joke.

YOSHITOKI (*after a deep silence, with a groan*): A joke . . . a joke, is that it?

(*The stage slowly darkens.*)

Scene Six

(*The sounds of the* WORKMEN *can be heard as the lights come up. The* WARRIORS *are seated in a circle around* SANETOMO *and* CHEN.)

SANETOMO (*spreading out the plans*): Of course Chen is certainly right when he says that if we make the ship larger, she will be harder to manipulate. But this is only a prob-lom in a cove or inlet. Along with the sails, we should plan on fifty oars. There are no Chinese vessels built along these lines, but in Japan large ships have always used oars of one kind or another. In the open sea a Chinese ship only has her sails to propel her. And our scheme will be helpful when our ship leaves harbor. Of course Chen feels a bit apprehensive about it. The ship will be that much heavier. If any mistake is made with the oars while in the harbor, a ship of two thousand stone will be in disastrous trouble. That much is true.

CHEN (*waving his hand*): That is not the only thing. A big ship is that much more dangerous in the open sea. The force of the waves comes in various places. The boat will twist. Split in the middle.

SANETOMO: For all I know you may be right. To prevent that, we'll have to make the keel thicker. And increase the number of supporting ribs. Actually, the other day I was presented with some splendid logs of camphor wood brought down from the mountains at Izu. From what I can see of the thickness and quality of the wood, they should do beautifully to make a keel, even for a ship of this size.

(*Several of the* WARRIORS *applaud.* AZUSA *enters without drawing any attention to herself, and remains behind the others.*)

SANETOMO: I must admit that I myself have never had complete confidence in our project. But the accidental gift of this wood seems a lucky omen. I'd like to make use of it and give one real try. I realize there are dangers. And I realize this new plan will greatly increase the labors we will have to perform. I put my absolute trust in you. What about it? Will you lend me your strength?

WARRIORS (*all rising at once*): We'll do it. Yes, let's do it.

SANETOMO: Thank you. Thank you, all of you. Chen Ho-ch'ing, I'm going to heighten the mast. I won't do anything imprudent. Come, let me show you the wood. (*He*

[159]

takes CHEN'S *hand and goes off at the back of the stage, taking the* WARRIORS *with him.* MIURA *and* KUGYŌ *now appear.)*

KUGYŌ (*lowering his voice*): The whole thing is becoming perfectly clear. Sanetomo's real desires have nothing to do with China. In fact, they don't even have anything to do with building that ship. The whole point is that to build a ship, you need lots of men. He can operate the whole scheme without any hindrance at all. This place will serve as a perfect spot, an intricate battlefield where he can train his men.

MIURA: I see. You mean to say that he is training his own private army?

KUGYŌ: As I watch his behavior these days, his intentions seem quite obvious. Giving alms for charity, making a show of his own courage, trying so hard to win the hearts of the people. Don't you see? What is hard for me to forgive is the fact that he has extended his own sordid hand to me in a gesture reconciliation. Become guardian of the Hachiman shrine? Ridiculous. What an insult to me, a direct descendant of the Minamoto family. Worst of all, he didn't even think of my situation until after he disposed of that lost brat he picked up.

MIURA (*agitated, blustering*): He's being hideously unfair. What frightening insolence.

KUGYŌ: Lord Miura, you, too, surely feel disgraced by all his ambiguous behavior. I used to think Sanetomo was the kind of man who lacked the will and the courage to take on an opponent properly, on the field of battle. I thought he was merely observing my comings and goings with that weak scornful smile on his face, like an old man peeping into other people's bedrooms. But things seem different now. He's setting out to really take the power of the Shōgun. And I'm the one standing in his way. Actually, Lord Miura, I now feel clear-headed, refreshed.

[160]

Even if Sanetomo continues to despise me, he can no longer smile that terrible smile. Because if, in his tenacity, he decides to do battle with me, he will find that my years of apprenticeship far outnumber his.

MIURA: I'm sure you're right. I must say, though, there's still one thing that bothers me. If Sanetomo wants to build up his own private army, then why does he go through the pretense of building a ship? After all, he's the Shōgun. If he wants to train a private army, why not go about it openly?

KUGYŌ: But that's quite obvious. He couldn't fully trust the regular soldiers, even under his own command.

MIURA: Yes. And I suppose Yoshitoki and Masako would study his every move. You're right. But even so, think a moment. What is the point of all that secret training?

(*The two look at each other.*)

KUGYŌ (*with an intake of breath*): Well, what do you think?

MIURA: It's just as you suggested. He intends to do battle with Yoshitoki. That's what he's planning.

KUGYŌ (*after a short silence, shaking his head vigorously*): No. No, Lord Miura, that's not it. That kind of idea is just too smooth. You have a bad habit. You use your head too much. That's why you miss good opportunities.

MIURA: Whatever you say, the essential thing for us to do is to break down that closeness between them. Well, I guess we'd better watch the situation a little longer. At some point, Sanetomo himself can certainly be put in his place.

KUGYŌ: Be careful. That's the whole trouble with any fancy scheme. A little inattention, and you'll find Sanetomo taking the initiative.

(*Their voices grow louder without their noticing,* SANETOMO *and* CHEN *enter noisily with the* WARRIORS *carrying lumber, carpenter's tools, etc.* AZUSA *then appears behind them, observing the situation.*)

[161]

SANETOMO: Good. I think we can use this scaffolding as it is. (*After giving his instructions to the* WARRIORS, SANETOMO *goes to speak with* KUGYŌ *and* MIURA, *who have lost their chance to escape.* SANETOMO *is beaming.*) Well, what a surprise to see the pair of you here. I had no idea you were interested in my ship.

MIURA (*assiduously changing his manner*): But have you forgotten, Lord Sanetomo? It is to us that you first revealed your plans to build a Chinese ship. And I must hasten to add that you have changed a great deal. At that time you used to defer to your mother's feelings. Now it seems you stand in awe of no one, but proceed on to do precisely what you wish.

SANETOMO: Oh, do you think so? Actually it seems to me that you are the one who has changed, Lord Miura. At that time you were terribly close with Wada Yoshimori. Of course, now I never see you together at all. . .

MIURA (*his face turning red with exasperation*): Thank you for your gracious words. I understand that since he's become a ghost, he sticks only to you.

SANETOMO: Actually, Lord Miura, ghosts have never really taken to me. And I'm sure I can't think why. (*He is teasing; and yet there is an element of quiet sincerity in his voice.*) When I wearied of talking with those who were alive, I used to think I would like to hear my revelations from ghosts. Because the dead ones have only their one crucial word to say, perhaps because they no doubt staked the most important thing in their life on that one word. A word of hatred or of trust. A single word that condenses a whole life. Oh, I was young then. When I was confused as to how to lead my life, I wanted to listen to them with great eagerness. Worthless. I spent whole long nights. There was no ghost anywhere who would say that one word to me.

KUGYŌ (*low, like a moan*): I heard them. A long, long time ago. I didn't want to hear them. I was forced to hear them.

[162]

SANETOMO (*with seriousness, gently*): Yes, I know. I can tell from looking in your eyes. I wonder which is worse: to have heard them, or not to have heard them.

(KUGYŌ *begins to speak, then swallows his words.*)

MIURA: Well, well. Your glory, Sanetomo, has put even the ghosts to rout, it seems. On the other hand, I understand that you find omens in your dreams. Which reminds me, do you really think that you will finally be sailing for China?

SANETOMO: Actually I'm still not certain. But if the ship can be constructed successfully, I may well do it.

MIURA: That too shows a change of heart. Before you said that the Shōgun himself must never be the one to search out any new country.

SANETOMO: Yes, but three years have passed since then. Kamakura is now calm, and the situation in the capital has quieted down as well. If I left for a year, even two years, the government would have no trouble.

MIURA: Yes, but China is far. What if, by some chance, something happened to you?

SANETOMO: So you think if something did happen to me, it would be only when I am not in Kamakura? Well, things have changed on that point too. Even if I were dead, now a splendid successor could be found.

(MIURA *and* KUGYŌ, *without thinking, stare at one another. Suddenly* YOSHITOKI *appears from the gloom behind the rear pillar, unnoticed.*)

MIURA (*restraining his nervousness, softly*): But I must ask you. In the case of such a situation, you feel that indeed a suitable successor. . .

SANETOMO (*laughing as if at a practical joke, plainly*): You really don't need to ask. Don't forget, Yoriie's little legacy Kugyō is still with us. You don't expect me to go around meddling in all that, do you? (*While talking,* SANETOMO *gives instructions to the* WARRIORS *and urges them on in their work.* KUGYŌ *stiffens, as if he had been struck.* YOSHITOKI *unconsciously steps forward to hear what is being said.*)

MIURA (*swallowing hard*): But surely, Lord Sanetomo . . . surely you are joking.

SANETOMO: A joke? Why should it be a joke? When I see you surprised to that extent, it almost seems you think Kugyō wouldn't make a suitable Shōgun. But actually, isn't the whole thing perfectly natural? I have no children myself. In any case, Kugyō is the only one with pure Minamoto blood flowing in his veins.

(MIURA *turns and looks at* KUGYŌ, *who in turn stares at* SANETOMO *without moving.*)

SANETOMO (*in a chatty voice, as he continues to direct the* WARRIORS *in their work*): There is, however, one piece of advice I do wish to pass on to Kugyō. You don't mind, do you Kugyō? Do not make yourself Shōgun. The role of Shōgun should be something given to you. You receive the appointment from others and it becomes your destiny to bring vitality to it. You can make a fool of yourself. The work is difficult. The hardest thing is finding the right means to use your energy properly.

(AZUSA *unconsciously steps forward, staring at* SANETOMO. WARRIORS *have already been tying together various large pieces of lumber and other materials to a rope coming down from the top of the stage.* SANETOMO *feels the rope and the materials with his hand, making sure they are properly prepared.*)

SANETOMO: If you push ahead recklessly, you're bound to get in someone's way. But if you decide to draw back, then everything loses vitality. Actually, the whole thing is like the job of the host who has invited guests to a banquet. If Kugyō becomes Shōgun he'll quickly understand for himself. But I can tell you that, even with this knowledge, the exertion of all this energy is a pretty tiring business.

(SANETOMO *climbs on top of the materials that have been tied together, then gives a signal to the* WARRIORS *holding the opposite end of the rope. They pull hard as* SANETOMO *and the lumber rise into the sky.*)

[164]

SANETOMO: When you go out hunting and there is no game
to be had, you may find great happiness in plucking the
flowers and grasses at the side of the road. Deeply involved in some momentous task, the act of straightening
things up in some little bookcase may be a source of deep
joy. I'm not talking about the kind of consciousness you
need to be a poet. If you want to be Shōgun, you've got
to forge your temperament, in just that way, so that you
can become a happy human being.

(*As the* WARRIORS *pull on the rope,* SANETOMO, *still talking, disappears above the proscenium. The noise of the construction
grows louder;* AZUSA, KUGYŌ, MIURA, *and* YOSHITOKI *look up in
silence as the lights fade.*)

Scene Seven

From the darkness comes the sound of AZUSA *singing a lullaby.
When the stage grows lighter, she can be seen dandling the* INFANT
on her knee as she continues to sing. After a moment, MASAKO
enters and stands behind her.)

MASAKO: Well, Azusa. I'm surprised to see how you've
changed. You used to find the work with the orphans
disagreeable. Now I see you are throwing yourself into
it.

AZUSA: You see, they are my children.

MASAKO: Your children. I see. From one point of view,
though, my son played a cruel joke on you. Because you
wanted children, he provided you with dozens of coun-
terfeits.

AZUSA: Yes. Of course you are right. And, from one point of
view, that is a brilliant bit of irony.

MASAKO: You certainly seem calm about the whole thing.
Hugged by an imposter, singing your little lullaby. Altogether devoted.

AZUSA: Look what my husband is doing. With all his devotion. Praying in the rain. Building a huge, huge ship . . .

MASAKO: You are cynical about my son. Or are you making insinuations against us all?

AZUSA: No. No I'm not. Perhaps I really have changed. These days, when I watch Sanetomo working to construct his ship, I have lost any feelings of sarcasm I might have had. He really seems deeply happy. I've come to think that it doesn't matter whether there is any ultimate meaning to what he does or not. I can watch the energy welling up from his body, time after time. I don't pretend to understand what is going on inside his heart, but from what I can see, I suddenly find myself persuaded.

(MASAKO *looks at* AZUSA, *as if she finds something suspicious. The lights dim.*)

Scene Eight

(*The lights come up below the platform as* YOSHITOKI *reads aloud.*)

YOSHITOKI: From 1215 through the early months of the following year, Sanetomo urged his warriors on as the work on the ship reached its climax. During this time, Sanetomo's usual visits to the Hachiman shrine were greatly increased in frequency. As Shōgun, his visits served a public function. But was he privately praying for something himself? There was, of course, no way to know. In the fourth month of 1217, the ship was finally completed, and its vast shape soared up from the sand on the shore at Yuigahama.

(*Light now falls on the upper platform.* MIURA *and* KUGYŌ *rush in.*)

MIURA (*rather excited*): So, tomorrow then. We'll find out everything tomorrow. We'll know if he really intends to sail to China, or not.

KUGYŌ: Well even if you find out, then what? While you go on making your endless plans, time, valuable time, has gone on, year after year.

MIURA: You're wrong. Waiting has turned out to be quite useful. Look at the maneuvers of the Emperor in Kyoto. Members of the court are again being banished to Kamakura. The Emperor seems determined to subjugate the Hōjō family. If Sanetomo leaves Kamakura for two years, a terrible war is bound to break out. And if that happens, the Hōjō, without a Shōgun, will have no appeal for these Eastern warriors.

KUGYŌ: And . . . if he doesn't go . . .

MIURA: Yoshitoki for one would be delighted. But what about those warriors Sanetomo has been working with so hard all these past months? They believe in his ambitions. They've given their energy, their hearts. Won't they feel cheated? Abandoned by his closest retainers, having lost the trust of everyone: that's precisely when you must show your strength and overthrow him.

KUGYŌ: It's certainly taken you a long time, but I see you, too, finally, have used those words "overthrow him."

MIURA: That's because he has changed. But this is hazardous talk. He has begun his political maneuvers. Do you remember what he said? He put the idea of the succession in your ear, as a means to begin driving a wedge between us.

KUGYŌ: Fascinating. I've seen worry on your face for the first time. Well. Don't worry. After all, who is the one who has been cheated? He means to play with me right to the bitter end.

(*The lights on the platform shift as* SANETOMO *and* CHEN *enter.* CHEN *paces around nervously.*)

CHEN: I do not know. I do not. Do you really intend to go on board? Do you plan to board her and sail across the sea?

SANETOMO: What a nuisance you are. Of course I do. (SANE-

[167]

TOMO, *muttering something to himself, pulls one leaf after another from a stalk he holds in his hand.*)

CHEN: But you must not. It is not a ship. It is an apparition. A ship of two thousand stone. What is more, you had three cabins built. The prow of the ship is too heavy. Too dangerous. And the weights in the bottom have been increased three times over. That is bad. So unreasonable. Sailing a ship like that you will sink, even on a fair day. Please. Sanetomo. Listen to what I tell you.

SANETOMO: To sink . . . Not to sink . . . Sink . . . Not to sink . . . (*Preoccupied,* SANETOMO *continues to pull off the leaves. The lights shift and illuminate* MASAKO *and* YOSHI-TOKI.)

MASAKO: Now what do you plan to do? If you hold back now, that child will board his ship and sail away. Today is the launching. Since morning the beach has been filled with herds of soldiers and horses, jostling together.

(*The clamor of voices can be heard in the distance.*)

YOSHITOKI (*after a brief silence*): I've made up my mind. I've decided to let him go. Wherever he wants to go.

MASAKO: I'm surprised. Your politics evidently no longer require a Shōgun to manipulate.

YOSHITOKI: I'm extremely apprehensive. Apprehensive that a young man, so wise, and so sensitive, can be made into a doll totally responsive to my will. Last night I talked alone with him here. And I understood. He is an intelligent boy. True, sometimes he has opposed me, sulked a bit perhaps, but in fact he has walked the path I laid out for him without so much as deviating one step.

MASAKO (*soothingly*): So indeed you do not covet him. If I think who Sanetomo most resembles, it may well be you yourself.

YOSHITOKI (*forcefully*): There is strength of purpose in me. I will not lose to the Emperor in Kyoto. I have a will to see this country governed in my own style.

MASAKO: And I suppose that the fact you are so taken by the boy shows that there must be some similarity between you.

YOSHITOKI: But my dear sister, aren't you perturbed? What if the boy has no such will himself? What if behind that face, which becomes angry, which laughs, like any man's, what if there is nothing at all behind it?

MASAKO: How complicated all this becomes. At the moment, I'm more worried about you than about Sanetomo.

YOSHITOKI:
"The world itself
   Is but a reflection in a mirror:
      If it seems to be there, it is,
         If not, then there is nothing."

That is one of Sanetomo's poems. I'm not sure I quite understand the part about being there and not being there. But if the whole world is just a reflection, where does that leave us, my dear sister? If Kamakura, the Emperor himself, if everything is an illusion, then all my strength evaporates. And more awesome is the man who can go on existing, serene, knowing that everything is an illusion. A man who conducts his life with good sense, and without despair, even though nothing, nothing at all makes any difference. With such a strong man nearby I am overwhelmed. I lose the strength to go on living.

MASAKO: Calm yourself, Yoshitoki. You are overanxious. You are very tired.

YOSHITOKI: Now I have only one hope. It is Sanetomo's ship. Because this is the only time he has positively opposed me. The one time he has stepped off the path I prepared for him. And with so much passion. Masako, we will allow him to do it. I want to see it. I want to see him once, firm in the belief that this world is not merely an illusion.

MASAKO (*looking at* YOSHITOKI *intently*): Of course. Decide things as you will. Because your feelings are now the important thing. Because we may allow some change in that boy. But none in you.

YOSHITOKI (*suddenly brightening*): And I've had another wonderful inspiration. Why not use this occasion to send our credentials to the Emperor of China? Even if harassed and weakened by the Barbarians to her North, China is a great country. If Kamakura and China could join hands, we could truly strike fear into the heart of the Emperor in Kyoto.

MASAKO: A splendid idea, I'm sure. Now you begin to seem yourself again. If it were not so, I'd be worried. Those quarrels with Kyoto will last a long, long time. In fact, what really disturbs me at the moment is the conduct of Miura Yoshimura. You know that recently there have been all sorts of visitors from the capital slipping in and out of his quarters. If we don't strike soon, we risk a repetition of the Wada incident all over again.

YOSHITOKI: I suppose you're right. But don't forget that the Miura family is very powerful. However unpleasant they may be, I hesitate to take them on. But I do see the problem. We must work out a strategy as rapidly as possible.

MASAKO: I'm absolutely delighted. Now you are really yourself. Your real self.

ŌE (*rushing in, all out of breath*): Be joyful! I have most heartening news. The ship . . . the ship won't move.

YOSKHITOKI (*astonished*): What? What's this?

ŌE: Yes, it's true. The ship will not move. There have been four hundred men and fifty horses assembled there, pulling. They've been at it more than half the day, but it won't move even a fraction of an inch. It is too heavy. It has sunk into the sand on the beach. How fortunate this is. Now Lord Sanetomo won't go anywhere.

YOSHITOKI: Grotesque . . . ridiculous. I'm going to see for myself. (*He begins to rush away.*)

[170]

ŌE: But . . . what is all this?

(ŌE *and* MASAKO *look at each other as the lights dim.*)

Scene Nine

The sound of distant commotion grows louder. On the platform, various sounds, including those of the agitated voices of the WARRIORS, *can be heard.*

WARRIORS: More horses! Hand over the rope! This way! This way!

(*As the lights come up, the* WARRIORS *can be seen moving busily about in the last glow of sunset. Against the central pillar a huge wooden wheel for coiling rope has been installed. The* WARRIORS *clutch the thick supports placed on all four sides. The rope is half coiled, and the other end of the line, absolutely taut, extends off stage. As* MASAKO, AZUSA, ŌE, *and* CHEN *watch*, YOSHITOKI *takes command.*)

YOSHITOKI: Pull it gently. That's it. That's right. You all have to fall into the same rhythm together. Watch my hand. Follow my signal. Are you ready? Wait now. Wait. Now, pull!

WARRIORS: *They all groan.*

(*As the* WARRIORS *begin to turn the wheel, the distant cries of men and the neighing of horses can be heard, along with the high-pitched sound of squeaking wood.*)

YOSHITOKI: Wait. It's no good. Wait.

CHEN (*clinging to* YOSHITOKI): No. This is not good. We have tried many times. So many times. Since morning. We tried a lever. We tried a roller. We dug a ditch. Underneath. Then we let the sea water flow in. No good. The ship did not float. Only sank further, into the ditch. What can we do? This is not my fault. Not my fault at all. Lord Yoshitoki, please try to understand.

YOSHITOKI: I understand perfectly. Keep out of my way. Come on everyone. More ropes have been added. I

[171]

promise you it will move this time. Let's try again. Make ready.

(KUGYŌ *and* MIURA *appear, astonished at what they see.*)

KUGYŌ (*whispering in* MIURA's *ear*): What on earth is going on? Uncle Yoshitoki has taken the lead, he's giving directions.

MIURA: He must be caught up in Sanetomo's enthusiasm. And look! (*Indicating a point off stage.*) Sanetomo is kneeling over there, praying as if his life depended on it.

KUGYŌ: With all this exaggerated excitement, if he gets that ship into the water, Sanetomo will have to set sail for China whether he wants to or not.

MIURA: And if the boat won't move, he may commit suicide out of discouragement.

YOSHITOKI (*with a bold gesture*): Everyone get ready now. Let's go.

(AZUSA *instinctively presses her hands together in prayer.* CHEN *covers his face.*)

YOSHITOKI: Pull!

WARRIORS: Ho!

YOSHITOKI: Pull!

WARRIORS: Ho!

(*The voices in the distance rise to a higher pitch. The ropes begin to wind with a terrible creaking.*)

WARRIORS: Ah! The ship has fallen over!

(AZUSA *screams; the far echo of the slow sound of rending and tearing is heard, followed by a terrible noise of breaking wood. The voices of* WARRIORS *and the neighing of horses grow more intense. All those on the stage remain where they are, staring vacantly.*)

CHEN: Ah! All broken to pieces. The bottom of the ship is all split open. Ah! The keel is broken too. Bad. Bad. This is the end. And I told him so. I told him.

(CHEN, *in agony, weeps. Suddenly the stage is quiet. All those on the stage stand as though petrified. A long silence.*)

WARRIOR 1: The Shōgun comes this way.

[172]

Sanetomo

(*The* WARRIORS *whisper together.* MASAKO *turns in the direction of* YOSHITOKI.)

MASAKO: Yoshitoki! The child has come. Are you ready? Pull yourself together.

(SANETOMO, *in a self-assured manner, walks slowly onto the platform. All instinctively shrink back.* SANETOMO, *facing* YOSHITOKI, *lowers his head silently.*)

YOSHITOKI: What a terrible shame. I am so sorry. I am so disappointed. More than anyone.

SANETOMO: Thank you, Uncle. But in any case, the whole thing is finished now. And mother, I am sorry that I caused you so much worry. (*In contrast to the pain in* YOSHITOKI's *voice,* SANETOMO's *seems exhuberant, bright.*)

YOSHITOKI (*shaking his head*): No. We are not finished yet. We will try again. And this time, I will work with you. I will help you.

SANETOMO: Thank you, Uncle. Really. But you needn't worry. For half a year I've been able to amuse myself to my heart's content. And I'm well satisfied.

YOSHITOKI: Sanetomo . . . (YOSHITOKI *cannot continue.* SANETOMO *is imperturbable.*)

SANETOMO: Thank you, everyone. You have worked so well for me, and for such a long time. True, the final result was unfortunate, but we all struggled hard together, and we had a wonderful time. We all worked together, and for the same idea. This is what made me happiest of all. For all the efforts you have made, I mean to ask my uncle for a generous reward for all of you. So then, let's disband. We will all return to our various stations, our various duties. From now on all of us will work for the good of Kamakura. (*All the* WARRIORS *drop their heads.* SANETOMO, *tapping those closest to him on the shoulder, prepares to leave.* MASAKO *comes forward.*)

MASAKO: Wait Sanetomo. Do you really intend to end all this here? You heard what your uncle said. He will be willing to help you, work with you another time.

[173]

SANETOMO (*with a buoyant smile*): To do the same thing again? There would be nothing interesting in that. And I have a great new undertaking that I must hurry to begin.

MASAKO: A new undertaking? What might that be?

SANETOMO (*looking somewhat self conscious*): Actually, I feel sure that at the court ceremonies in the coming year I will be promoted to the rank of Provisional Major Counsellor. Then, after that, I hope to become a Major Captain of the Inner Palace Guards, Left Division. And, if I can get that far, I can easily rise to the rank of Great Minister of the Right.

(*Only* AZUSA, *who seems delighted, comes forward.*)

ŌE (*in agitation*): But My Lord. This is impossible. These court ranks are not merely toys. These are dangerous amusements.

SANETOMO: I wonder. Remember, my ship was no mere toy. Do you think seeking high court rank is any more dangerous than building a ship?

ŌE: Your Lordship increased the size of the ship beyond its proper due. That's why it eventually broke to pieces.

SANETOMO: You may be right. But the point is I saw the whole thing through. That's why I can feel at peace about it now. Then, there remains the question of my poetry collection. Have some copies made and send them on to the capital. I'm particularly anxious that you send one to the Emperor, and one to the greatest poet at court, Fujiwara Teika. (*His eyes suddenly glittering.*) Of course! I have just obtained some splendid Chinese paper. It was sent on to me by a merchant living in the capital. Paper like that is scarcely ever seen, even there. Let us make the copy for Fujiwara Teika on that paper. Tomorrow we will arrange all the details, so do not fail to come to my apartments. Well, Azusa. We haven't had time to be together for so long. This evening we must relax and enjoy each other. So then, everyone. Good night!

[174]

Sanetomo

(*All are greatly surprised;* AZUSA *takes his arm energetically and they exit.* YOSHITOKI *begins to follow them but stops after two or three steps.*)

YOSHITOKI (*murmuring*):
"The world itself
Is but a reflection in a mirror:
If it seems to be there, it is,
If not, then there is nothing . . .
It is seems to be there it is,
If not, then there is nothing . . ."

Curtain

Epilogue

The stage is arranged exactly as in Act I, Scene 1. However, there is no yardarm on the pillar.
(SANETOMO, *wearing elaborate court dress, is leaning against the pillar looking up at the sky. A white, abstract light falls from above; below the platform drifts a faint yellow light in which all the other characters with the exception of* SANETOMO *can be seen crouching or standing, lost in their thoughts. There is brief music as the curtain rises, then* YOSHITOKI *begins speaking as though he were reading aloud.*)

YOSHITOKI: 1218. The year after Sanetomo's ship was left rotting on the beach. Sanetomo is now twenty-seven. Fifteen years have past since he was given the rank of Shōgun. This year, his rapid rise in court rank as well is remarkable. He was named Provisional Major Counsellor on the thirteenth day of the first month. On the sixth day of the third month, he was given concurrently the post of Major Captain of the Inner Palace Guards. Next, on the ninth day of the tenth month, he was elevated to the rank of Great Minister of the Center. Finally, on the twelfth day of the twelfth month, he attained the highest rank of all, Great Minister of the Right.

(*As the reading goes on,* WARRIORS *mount the platform one by one. They bring in turn belts, swords, maces, ceremonial head gear, etc., and hand them over one by one and have them fastened on. In the midst of a brilliant light, the figure of* SANETOMO *appears, dressed in the full regalia of his new rank of Great Minister of the Right.*)

YOSHITOKI: 1219. It is early in the morning of the twenty-seventh day of the first month.

WADA (*suddenly interrupting* YOSHITOKI): Lord Yoshitoki! You don't really have to tell this whole story right to the end. I've been watching everything so far, and I can tell you I'm pretty tired out. What happens from now on is really quite clear. Actually, the whole thing was quite an unremarkable sort of incident. There was snow that morning. Yes, I remember. Lord Sanetomo was paying a visit to the great Hachiman Shrine to thank the Gods for his ascension to the rank of Great Minister of the Right.

(*The light on the platform changes to suggest a snowy morning. In the sky behind a few flakes of snow begin to fall. Four* WARRIORS *accompany* SANETOMO. *They begin to walk slowly.* WADA, *as before, looks toward the audience and continues to speak.*)

WADA: But that day, for some reason or other, Yoshitoki found himself ill and declined to accompany Sanetomo on his pilgrimage. Why should it have been that Yoshitoki, who always stayed so close to Sanetomo, should on that very day . . .

(SANETOMO *and the four* WARRIORS *cross the platform in a formal gait, and passing between the two pillars, go to the rear.*)

KUGYŌ (*in a gloomy voice, picking up from* WADA): "For some reason or other?" We don't need to put on any airs. Uncle Yoshitoki knew exactly what would happen. He knew I would be hiding in the shade of the ginko tree in the shrine compound . . . Well, we don't need to say any more about that. I'm sick to death of the whole thing. How long is this stupid farce going to continue? Just as Lord Wada said, we certainly know how it's all going to come out. I pulled out my sword and rushed at him. What did I scream out at him? I don't remember myself. I recall I came down on him with my brandished sword and struck him dead.

(*At the back of the platform, a terrible scream from* SANETOMO. *Afterwards, a deep silence.*)

KUGYŌ (*all alone*): Then that same day, that very evening, I was killed by Lord Miura here.

(*The lights on the platform change again to the former abstract white.*)

MIURA (*continuing, in a voice that shows his annoyance*): Now the whole thing begins to seem pretty clear to me. Yoshitoki knew about lots more. He knew that I was behind the incident and had coaxed Kugyō to do what he did. Yoshitoki had positive proof. But he let me go ahead and do it. What a brilliant maneuver on his part. Why? Because he needed my strength in his war against the Emperor. He wanted to dazzle me with the proof. Frighten me. His plan was to have me attack his enemies in Kamakura, no matter how painful it was for me. Well, I have to respect him. I know I am an evil man, but my intelligence doesn't go as far as his. Well, what can you do? I hurried to his mansion with the severed head of Kugyō as a present.

YOSHITOKI (*filled with bitter irony, speaking as if delivering a soliloquy*): I feel only a sense of regret. I was exhausted.

[177]

All I can think is that I was under the influence of some evil spirit. Originally I had intended to stop Miura's grim plan before anything happened. I managed to grasp the progress of the incident moment by moment, but I withdrew for one fateful instant and merely watched the course of events . . . I have thought about all of this for some time now. For Sanetomo, the Shōgunate of Kamakura was just like his ship. Even when that ship rotted in the sand, he was perfectly composed, perfectly cheerful. And that being true, then why, when my Kamakura fell to pieces . . . But why did he act that way? Why? It was my thinking over and over that very point that made me so weary. The Sanetomo who presented me night and day with just this puzzle became too heavy a burden for me to bear. (*After a short silence, with strength.*) But still I wished that he might somehow come to his senses. I hoped that if I suddenly gave up the pilgrimage with the excuse of a sudden illness, he might realize something was amiss and turn back himself. It was no use. It was just like when he built his ship. That boy thrust out his chest, dressed in all his court robes, and walked right on up those snowy steps.

WADA (*rising, to console* YOSHITOKI): Everything's fine now, Lord Yoshitoki. Having acted out the story this far, we've come to understand each other's feelings, our real feelings, very well indeed. If we go any further, we will only open old wounds. We won't accomplish anything. That's enough. Anyway, no matter how long we continue, we still won't know the first thing about Sanetomo's true character.

(*Now* SANETOMO, *who has shed his headgear, sword, etc., and is wearing a simple hunting costume, returns to the platform. He holds a leafy stalk in his hand, and he whispers as he pulls off the leaves one by one.*)

SANETOMO: Right, left, right, left. Live, die, live, die, live . . . Hey! Lead the horse properly. I'm going hunting, after all. Why don't we send a huge wild boar to the capital and frighten the Emperor? (*He throws the stem away, smiling happily.*)

KUGYŌ (*before the platform, in great agitation*): I can't stand it anymore. I just can't bear it. Why doesn't he come down here with the rest of us? Look, look at him. He's still up there. He should get right down here and let us hear from his own lips the truth about everything. What has he been thinking? What kind of man was he?

YOSHITOKI (*lightly, a note of self-scorn in his voice*): Ever since the day the ship was wrecked, I have asked myself time and time again how to get a hold on that boy. And the answer has always been the same.

(*On top of the platform,* SANETOMO *talks as if addressing an invisible partner.*)

SANETOMO: But why won't you believe me? I am just an ordinary man. I'm not trying to tell you any lies. I'm not acting out a play. When Wada Yoshimori died, I was truly grieved, from the bottom of my heart. But my uncle's concept of politics excited me. And I was fascinated to the same degree by the role of Shōgun bequeathed to me by my uncle.

KUGYŌ (*stamping furiously on the floor*): That's why I'm telling you to get down here with the rest of us. Then you can tell us what your motives really were, and bow your head. But as long as you stay up on that false platform, I can't hear anything in what you say but tricks to hoodwink us.

MIURA (*bantering*): Don't waste your breath. He'll never come down here. Do you really think that a man who cannot separate work and pleasure can have any purpose, any real intention?

MASAKO (*still crouching*): Give the whole thing up. As far as I'm concerned, I don't need to understand the child anyway. He did a lot of foolish things, but he was a loyal son in the end. His poems earned him quite a reputation,

[179]

and he did manage to get to the rank of Great Minister of the Right. And he was a great help to me at times. Why bother to understand what he was thinking? After all, whatever you may say, I'm the one who bore him.

YOSHITOKI (*muttering absentmindedly*):
"If not, there is nothing . . .
   If it seems to be, there is . . .
      If not, then there is nothing . . ."

AZUSA (*rising slowly*): I am the one who killed him. With all the passion in my nature I urged Sanetomo to take me, to possess me fully. I should have been just the opposite. I am the one who should have taken him into my possession. But I became aware of this too late. (*Suddenly, with great force.*) I have a request to make of all of you. Do not end all this in such a mournful way. For my sake, my sake, show me the scene. Where the sails are raised on Sanetomo's ship.

(*Great commotion from all.*)

MIURA (*shaking his head*): Well, I don't know about that. I don't think our agreement includes doing anything like that. After all, such a scene never existed.

KUGYŌ (*hurriedly tidying himself up*): I have to bow out of this one. I don't feel like trying to go through with something I know all too well never came about.

AZUSA: All of you. Please do this for me. Anyway, it's only a foolish dream of mine. After all, you wouldn't make him any more a hero, just by doing this.

(*A moment of silence.*)

YOSHITOKI (*coming forward*): Let's do it. Not for the sake of Azusa or Sanetomo. But for me.

(SANETOMO *lifts his right hand and all the* WARRIORS *rush on the stage. They quickly attach the yard to the central pillar and pull the ropes out. The lighting changes. A bright deep blue sky appears.* CHEN HO-CH'ING *comes happily to* SANETOMO.)

[180]

Sanetomo

CHEN: All preparations have been made for the sailing. Please, give the order!
(SANETOMO, *consenting, walks to the front of the platform. Suddenly the sounds of waves and wind well up.*)
SANETOMO: Check the wind!
WARRIOR 1: A good wind. A tail wind.
SANETOMO: Check the tide.
WARRIOR 2: The tide is good.
SANETOMO: The yardarm ready?
WARRIOR 3: Ready!
SANETOMO: The sail ropes ready! The anchor chain ready!
WARRIOR 4: Ready!
WARRIOR 5: Ready!
(*As* SANETOMO *quickly raises his hand,* KUGYŌ *mutters just loudly enough to be heard.*)
KUGYŌ: I'm overwhelmed. He's really putting everything he's got into it. In the middle of a senseless dream, when he knows nothing will come of it, why does he never become discouraged? Why?
YOSHITOKI (*smiling happily*): There is one thing that does seem certain. There may be no other world at all. But in this one, Sanetomo is a man who, through his own inner strength, will live out his life without ever losing heart.
SANETOMO (*crying out with great intensity*): Lift the anchor! Hoist the sails!
WARRIORS: Ho! Ho!
(*On the mast, pure white sails billow up, filled by the wind. Music. The area before the platform darkens completely. From that darkness a chorus of whispers begins.*)
VOICES: Sanetomo, Sanetomo, Sanetomo . . .

Curtain

[181]

An Interview
with Yamazaki Masakazu

While Sanetomo *was being produced in St. Louis in April 1976, I had occasion to talk at length with Mr. Yamazaki about his own career and about various aspects of the contemporary theater in Japan. His answers were always stimulating and highly informative. The text is included here as a source of additional information for readers interested in his work. A slightly different version appeared in the summer 1977 issue of* The Denver Quarterly, *vol. 12, no. 12.*

Some Personal Details

TR: Your own personal background is unusual, in that you spent your young years outside of Japan. Do you think that this early cosmopolitan experience gave you (like Thornton Wilder, for example) any special impetus toward literature and the theater?

YM: I am still not certain what the influences may have been on my writing resulting from the fact that I spent my childhood in northwestern China, in the area formerly called Manchuria. I lived there from the age of six to the age of twelve. Whatever those influences may have been, they were surely subconscious, for my full consciousness of the whole experience was certainly to come later. One thing I certainly can say, though, is that my appreciation of nature is not typically Japanese. I don't particularly care for cherry blossoms; I feel more of a closeness for lilacs, and to poplar and elm trees. In 1963, when I first visited New England, I was delighted to find again such plants and trees, so familiar to me as a child.

On the other hand, the experiences I underwent when Manchuria collapsed were fundamental in my own development. My whole view of life was profoundly changed. In terms of providing material for my own writing I became interested not, say, in portraying delicate psychological burdens within a family; rather, I was captivated by the idea of a theater in which a man's fate could be thrust directly onto the stage of history.

TR: When did you first begin to take an interest in the theater? Was this your first literary interest, or did you find yourself attracted to other aspects of literature first? How did your interest develop?

YM: My first clear memory of my involvement with the theater remains that of the winter when I was twelve years old. My father was ill, on the verge of death. I sat at his pillow and read to him the works of Shakespeare in the Tsubouchi Shōyō translation. Manchuria had fallen. It was the period when both Nationalist and Communist troops were occupying the country. The streets were full of those dead from cold or starvation. Even in our own home only the stove in my father's sick room could be kept burning. Under such circumstances this book of Shakespeare remained the only item of literature on our bookshelves. With the sound of cannons booming in the distance, I watched my father's face, from which consciousness seemed slowly to be fading even as I read to him. *Coriolanus, Henry IV, The Tempest* . . . I certainly didn't understand every word that I read there. Yet my reading those plays aloud seemed somehow a suitable way to attack the miseries of reality through the strength that the words of Shakespeare's strong imagination gave to me.

TR: Did you take up the formal study of drama while a student?

YM: After the death of my father I returned to Japan and lived in Kyoto during my high school and college years. During that time it seems to me that I consciously avoided having much to do with literature. I suppose my attitude was one common to young people: while I had a strong fascination with the movements of the human personality, I was easily fatigued by such complex difficulties, and the image of emotional turbulence was one I found distasteful. I felt the emotional element in the human personality might be abandoned and that the use of reason might suffice to solve our problems. At first I took an interest in the social sciences, then later I took up the study of philosophy with an emphasis on phenomenology. It then became clear to me that no escape might free one from the oppression of the emotions and that the only possibility for deliverance would be to find a way in which that emotion might be expressed in a certain artistic form, as R. G. Collingwood suggested. About the time I graduated from Kyoto University I found myself attracted again to literature. This time it was again to the drama that I gave my attention. I felt convinced at the time that, unlike the novel, the drama can portray men in their outward aspects; the undulations of interior subjective emotion are not immediately touched upon. I found myself altogether satisfied with a form of literature that can capture in outline an emotion made apparent through action. The first play I wrote was called *Ite chō* (Frozen Butterfly), in one act, with four characters. The dialogue continued unabated for more than two hours! The play was performed both in Kyoto and Kobe, but I suspect that actors and audience alike felt as much fatigue as pleasure in their participation. If nothing else, I certainly learned from this experience to allow enough time for the audience (to say nothing of the actors) to go and have a smoke or to use the restroom! But of course I was only twenty-two and knew nothing of the actual conditions of the theater.

Since that time, eight volumes of my long plays and two of my one-act plays have appeared, and my dramas have also been staged in Tokyo and elsewhere.

The Artist in the Theater

TR: How are your plays produced?

YM: Ordinarily I begin to write a play on commission from a theater troupe. The demand for new dramas is always high, since ordinarily a play can only find an audience for somewhere between seven and fifteen performances. Ironically such circumstances cause the creation of more and more plays. Once I accept the commission and begin to plan my text, I consult fully with the producers, the director, and his other associates concerning the main themes and elements involved in my central conception. Once I begin to write, however, I take advice from no one, nor do I have many opportunities either during rehearsals or after the play has opened, to rewrite my text on the basis of the reactions of the actors or the audience.

TR: Nevertheless, have you ever revised any of your plays after seeing them on the stage?

YM: When I give my text to the actors it usually goes to a publishing house at the same time. I can't manage to create two separate plays with one title at the same time! I can make changes in the text only after the first production of a play is long finished and I am lucky enough to anticipate a second and new production. Such changes were made, for example, when *Zeami* was produced in Italy seven years after its Tokyo production and when

[186]

Sanetomo was given its American production four years after it was seen in Japan. In any case, no matter what my impressions may be when I see my plays staged, or whatever the reactions of my audiences might be, a certain amount of time must pass before I can obtain any objective view of my own work.

TR: A number of your most successful plays involve elements drawn from Japanese (or in some cases Western) history. What draws you to the use of history?

YM: For me, the plot and the *mythos* of a drama must always be separated. The plot serves to provide the framework of the play and in its construction must show originality, but the *mythos*, which provides the thematic material that the plot merely serves to explicate, must remain universal, transcending any merely personal level of understanding. The theater must create a dialogue between the stage and the spectators. In order for that conversation to develop in a rich and active way the topic, the "space" in which that conversation begins, must represent something shared. The *mythos* provides precisely that communality. For that reason, too, myth, legend, history, or even some well-known contemporary incident can serve those purposes most effectively. For this reason I have often used for my own plays incidents taken either from European or Japanese history. I wrestle with an image "shared in common"; then, taking this image as my ground, my own personal vision can begin to manifest itself.

Then again, the use of history as the basis for drama permits the author to maintain a necessary psychological distance from the world of his play while also helping him to create that world with a proper density, in neither too precise nor too abstract a fashion. To put it another way, if one writes without recourse to history, in an attempt to portray the contemporary world directly, one risks on the one hand the danger of losing oneself in the

[187]

creation of endless detail concernng psychological reactions and attitudes or, on the other hand, the danger of creating merely some allegory based on a lifeless and abstract idea.

TR: Do your audiences find such a use of history appealing? Can you assume they have the necessary background to follow the plays?

YM: Unfortunately audiences in Japan are scarcely well-prepared for dramas based on historical subjects. Since the Second World War, the teaching of history in Japan has stressed a so-called "scientific" approach to its subject matter with a resulting emphasis on economic and social analysis. The role of the individual act in history has been slighted. Most younger members of the audience have little knowledge of the more traditional historical facts a playwright might choose to use as a background for his conceptions. For example, fifteen years ago, when *Zeami* was first produced in Tokyo, there were university students who could not even decipher the names of the characters in the play—the names of those who founded the *nō* drama—written in the usual Chinese ideographs.

In the middle of the 1960s, however, popular magazines began to show a renewed interest in history and the schools too began to make up for their former deficiencies. Educational television produced programs dealing with the biographies of historical individuals, and popular historical novels began to prevail. All of these were well-received by broad segments of the population. In a certain sense, then, conditions for a drama based on history have improved during the last ten years. Nevertheless, I always work to make the historical background of my plays as clear as possible. My play *Sanetomo*, for example, involves a theme that certainly demands a highly theatrical treatment. The play doubtless evolved into the form it finally took because the historical facts themselves could be simply and clearly explained. For all those reasons, it is my hope that these historical plays of mine, even though they deal with the Japanese past, may be easy to comprehend even by foreign readers or spectators. Here is hopefully one example of the fact that, in the world of art, difficult conditions do not merely represent a hindrance to creation.

TR: Whatever the setting or background of your plays, however, the philosophical concerns of your drama seem strikingly contemporary.

YM: When I write a play or, for that matter, a literary essay of any sort, I certainly do not have any intention of stressing any formed set of philosophical principles. However I must say that I harbor strong doubts concerning the modern conception of the ego—that is to say, the concept of a fundamental element, continuous, unchanging. This modern view somehow supposes that an individual will, vis-a-vis another, always possess a sense of himself and, moreover, will continuously maintain a logical grasp of his own intellectual and emotional reactions. Such a view seems to presuppose that the requirements for human life remain consistent. Yet such a concept of the existence of the self (which parallels the concept of a unique God in a religion such as Christianity) can only be posited as a mode of human existence under certain, and rather exceptional, circumstances. I find no necessary connection between a man's consciousness of his subjective "being" and some objective "ego" with a substantial existence. Indeed the substance of this "ego," either in terms of feeling or of thought, only finds its reality when that individual manifests himself in the external world; and such a manifestation cannot take place without recourse to a connection with other human beings. More simply said, the "ego" cannot merely exist within a human being, only when that individual is in contact with others. Such a fact makes the base for the ego a

[189]

most unsteady one. For it is rare that others can correctly grasp the real motives of an individual. And it is rarer still for most human beings to possess a consistent understanding of what such an essential personality might be.

Even if a second person can recognize the concept of a particular individual's consistent human personality, he will form an image of that individual's personality in terms of categories of "common sense" and generally-accepted ideas, categories and ideas that have little connection with the ever-fluid and individual image that the individual has of himself. Yet insofar as an individual wishes to be true to himself, he must of necessity disregard the image the others conceive of him. He must rather manifest the image that seems true to him in each particular instant, thus destroying the "common sense" understanding that the others have of him.

In one sense it may be well that the ego represents merely the outcome of the curious and contradictory urges of the individual. It seems as if two conflicting human urges join together: the desire to find one's existence as an organism that changes in each passing moment, and the hope to find some kind of eternal self. The sense of the "ego" surely arises from this. Yet it is not permitted any living being to fix its existence permanently; there is only the fusing, the melting of the "stream of consciousness" proposed by Bergson and James, a state that absolutely precludes any hope of eternalization. Nevertheless a belief that those contradictory impulses can somehow be unified has developed, particularly in the West, from the eighteenth to the middle of the nineteenth century. Today this belief is questioned in a variety of ways. More and more the incertitude concerning any definition of human "identification" is discussed more and more openly, more and more despairingly. For the individual this uneasiness, this incertitude represents the very basis of existence, in my view.

An Interview with Yamazaki Masakazu

Looking back over my past work it now seems clear to me that, without purposely setting out to do so, I have somehow reflected through the themes of my plays, from *Zeami* onwards, my lack of trust in this modern conception of the ego. Most of the major characters I have created do not believe in their own ideas or in their own social positions, nor do they feel that their past has fully determined their present. Nor do they hold any firm convictions concerning their own future hopes. Nevertheless, I worked hard, both in *Sanetomo* and in *Zeami*, to indicate my belief that such men are neither nihilistic nor cynical in their attitudes. For me, such men are by no means unique or exceptional. What seems unique, rather, remains the existence of those men who continue to hold a belief in the continuity of their own personalities, those men who remain the product of the influences of that special age that began with Descartes and ended with Stendhal.

TR: Why do you find these concerns best expressed in the form of drama?

YM: Let me give you one example. My play *Sanetomo* was written under the influence of *Hamlet*. Yet if we take *Hamlet* as a representative of seventeenth-century man, he certainly had no "ego" in the modern sense of the word. Indeed he presents a most typical human image. If you search with care you can discover men like him who appear in countless plays written ever since the time of the Greeks. In that sense, then, I did not take the character of Hamlet as the "subject" of my play; in fact you might say that the existence of such a personality remains the premise on which I have written all my plays.

Of course such a human personality can be portrayed in any form of literature, but I think drama remains the most effective vehicle. First of all, because a drama is built on conversations, and secondly because the role of the actor also enters in. In a drama, dialogue replaces the words of a narrator in fiction; the speeches of no character can be taken as absolute. Whatever one character may say can be either contradicted, corrected, or sustained by the words of another. The impression is therefore easy to create: any real truth that exists must be relative. Again, one character may view the world in a particular fashion, but it will be viewed by others quite differently: thus the self-image or ego of that character may be controlled by means of such other views. During the course of a drama we can watch as a man tries, in front of the others, to construct his own self-image, and we can witness as well the difficulties, indeed the vanity, of such an effort.

The actor, for his contribution, helps heighten the sensibilities of the audience so that they too can come to understand that the ego of the character represented on the stage is not merely flat, not merely an "essence." Certainly if a man who really resembled Hamlet saw even John Gielgud in the part, he would certainly feel that he was merely watching a performance on the stage and that this theatrical Hamlet could not represent the character in totality. Inside any man there exists the "he" he plays himself and the "he" actually played; in the drama, because of its very nature as an art form, this profound fact of human existence is rendered comprehensible. The playwright who remained most highly conscious of this function of the theater and who made the best use of it was, of course, Pirandello.

TR: In writing plays that involve historical characters, men such as Zeami and Sanetomo, men whose lives and artistic works are well-known, do you attempt to stay close to the historical facts? Or, to put it another way, do you use these characters as pretexts for speculations on the meaning of the present as we understand it? To what extent is historical validity of interest to you? What kind of "aesthetic distance" from the present can the use of such characters provide?

YM: In dealing with historical subjects, I always try to in-

[192]

terpret the facts. But I have never ventured to forge one! In both *Zeami* and *Sanetomo,* for instance, all the dates, the names of the characters portrayed, the episodes shown, and the artistic works quoted, are correct historically or, at least, as faithfully rendered as they can be in terms of our own present knowledge of the past. I create particular episodes in these plays within the limits imposed by the main lines of the established biography of the personality concerned. The views on aesthetics revealed by Zeami in the course of the play reflect quite precisely what he himself wrote concerning his theories on art and the role of the artist. For me, the use of such historical material has a particular benefit. It is not that I wish merely to take advantage of the freedom they permit my imagination. On the contrary, such materials provide me with a resistant framework to challenge my imagination. In other words, I do not use the past as a means to speculate on the present. I try to use my contemporary sensibility to search out the meanings, the implications of the past.

TR: Both *Zeami* and *Sanetomo* use artists as main characters. Are there not peculiar problems involved in creating art about art? Is there not a risk that, under such circumstances, the plays of Zeami and the poetry of Sanetomo may be reduced to mere "objects" in the play and so lose their power?

YM: The most fundamental problem, of course, lies in the impossibility of actually showing on the stage the scenes in which these artists demonstrate their own creativity. It would take Zeami himself to permit my audience to witness a performance by "Zeami" on stage. And it would make a farce out of my tragedy should I try to depict Sanetomo composing his poem while shaking his head and walking back and forth in his garden. In view of such difficulties, I am careful to avoid using artistic works as materials for my plays. Rather I try to take from

[193]

such works the aesthetic and philosophic view of the world they provide. Such becomes my subject. In Western drama there is perhaps a certain parallel to offer in the dramaturgy of the classic French theater, in which, although the most overtly dramatic incidents—murders, suicides, love affairs—are not shown on stage, the fate of the men and women who inhabit these dramas is clearly represented.

TR: Who are the dramatists who had been most influential on your own work?

YM: The playwright who, both in his conception of man and in his theatrical manifestation of that conception, has influenced me most is Shakespeare. Among Japanese dramatists, surely Zeami: yet what I learned from him concerns the basic principles of the drama, particularly as regards his view of mankind that one finds concentrated there. In terms of particular techniques of playwriting, however, I have as yet learned little from the *nō*. Among the modern dramatists I admire most I must indicate Pirandello and Chekhov, but I have not borrowed consciously any theatrical techniques from their works. Pirandello taught me to hold the artistic point of view that "a play is a play, not a reflection of reality." Chekhov gave me an image of theatrical figures who, during the course of a drama, continue to search for themselves while all the while wearying of that same search.

TR: What significance have you found, as a practicing playwright, in *kabuki, nō,* and *bunraku?*

YM: I have never taken anything whatsoever from *kabuki* and *bunraku.* When I wrote *Zeami,* I borrowed several episodes from Zeami's own plays, but nothing whatsoever of his dramatic style, for this style is closely allied to the style in which such drama is performed. To separate the two and to try to give life to such traditional forms of drama would be difficult indeed. Yet, in the future, such experiments might have some value. For example, in the

[194]

nō, many plays are constructed in two parts. In the first part, for example, a warrior might appear in the manifestation of an old farmer. In the second part he will reveal his real form and recount his tragic experiences. In such a dramatic pattern one protagonist bears two identities, and the contrast between these two identities provides a powerful theatrical effectiveness. Such a form might well find some application in the contemporary theater.

Nor is this protagonist with differing or multiple identities confined to the *nō;* similar characteristics can be found throughout the traditional Japanese theater. In *kabuki* and *bunraku,* for example, the protagonist often actually represents the apparition of a monster who, because of whatever circumstances may be involved, disguises himself with the name and the appearance of a man. Of course there are many examples of this phenomenon in Western theater as well. In Shakespeare's *Twelfth Night,* to choose an obvious example, the protagonist is disguised as another person. In *Oedipus Rex* of Sophocles, two personalities lie within the protagonist, that of "the great king" and that of "the dishonored criminal." Such double personalities are invariably effective on the stage. In fiction, too, there are such accounts, and on the most popular level, too, such as *Dr. Jekyll and Mr. Hyde.* The pattern is surely one of universal application.

In the case of the Japanese theater, however, this piling up of multiple personalities does not exist merely for the purposes of dramatic conflict; indeed, this piling up does not accompany such conflict but actually *forms* the central element in the drama. It seems to me that, theatrically speaking, such a mode of viewing the structure of character remains a unique feature of traditional Japanese drama, and one that might well be made use of in our contemporary theater.

TR: Hopefully, *Zeami* and *Sanetomo* will give English-speaking readers some idea of the depth and range of your ac-

[195]

complishments as a playwright. What other of the plays that you have written would you like to see translated? Why?

YM: There are many; but in particular I would like most to see translated my *Oh, Heloise!,* which I wrote in 1972. It seems to me that, since I dealt there with a Western legend, that of Abelard and Heloise, whatever might represent my "Japanese" style or sensibility would be more conspicuous to a Western audience, separated from any "Japaneseness" in the subject matter itself.

TR: Your intellectual activities are far-ranging: you have written in the past few years on aesthetics, Mori Ōgai, contemporary American life, and half a dozen other subjects. Do you find these concerns divorced from your work in the theater, or do these concerns interact?

YM: Comparatively speaking, American intellectuals pursue one specialty more deeply than do their Japanese counterparts. Japanese show broader interests and are obliged to work effectively within a wider sphere. The lives of Japanese intellectuals are excessively busy, and I cannot deny that the risk always remains, therefore, that the contents of their work will remain superficial. On the other hand, don't you find a general tendency now for intellectuals all over the world to broaden their interests? Individual specialized intellectual methodologies are now being overturned. Certainly in the case of French intellectuals, such has been the tendency since early in the century, when men with diverse talents such as Malraux, Marcel, and Sartre chose central methodologies applicable to every aspect of their lives, methodologies that shaped each of their whole characters, both intellectually and emotionally. In my own case, my sensitivity to the theater, in the very broadest possible sense of the word, provided me with a set of attitudes that functions in somewhat the same fashion. When I write a literary essay, or a biography, I seldom choose a subject toward

[196]

which I feel either highly sympathetic or for which I feel any antagonism. Perhaps I might say that I usually feel an ambivalence toward the object I study. I attempt to put aside any subjective emotions I may feel; I look rather for subjects that permit theatrically-effective dialogue.

The History of the Modern Theater in Japan: A Status Report

TR: Japanese critics and historians of the theater are always quick to point out how short the history of the New Theater Movement actually is. Yet after all, Antoine, who is usually given credit for the beginning of a real movement for a modern theater in Europe, only began his work in Paris twenty years or so before that of Osanai Kaoru in Japan. Why, then, did the movement take so long to get under way after Osanai's first brilliant beginnings?

YM: First of all, it is important to remember that Antoine's idea of a modern theater found deep roots in the European tradition, especially in the French classical drama. Such basic principles of dramaturgy, such as the logical development of a theme, the rational construction of plot, and the importance of the psychological identity of the characters, even the presence of the proscenium stage, all of these were already prepared for Antoine. They formed his inheritance from the so-called "boulevard theater." None of this tradition was available either to Osanai or to his audience. For them, the introduction of a modern theater did not mean an evolution. It represented a total dislocation of their theatrical sensibilities.

In addition to such basic difficulties, the historical and sociological factors that prevented a healthy and a rapid development of a modern Japanese theater must be cited. First of all, the relative poverty of Japan during the last hundred years must be taken into consideration. Added to that is the vital importance of the kind of moralistic framework in terms of which those generations led their lives. Since the beginning of the Meiji Period [1868], Japan found herself in a most difficult international climate and was forced to industrialize with the greatest possible rapidity. All the funds available had to be used as capital for such projects. In the cultural sphere as well the most essential efforts went toward the building of schools, then for the development of the mass printing of books dealing with various new educational materials.

Additional factors as well need to be cited. In the preceding Edo Period [1600–1868] literacy in Japan spread rapidly and broadly, and the population as a whole took great interest in books designed for school instruction. From the seventeenth century onwards, increasing numbers of schools for primary education were constructed in all parts of the country, and the printing of popular books for amusement purposes became an important business. The development of such national habits—pleasure in reading and finding value in the production of books as a cultural phenomenon—can be verified by observing that, in the early nineteenth century, popular national magazines were established.

The development of the theater, however, stands in considerable contrast. Certainly the theater in the Edo period was quite active. Yet as an institution it never received public recognition and support. In France and England, for example, the Court publicly supported the theater as a place for entertainment. In the case of *kabuki*, however, there could be no question whatsoever of any connection with the Court; indeed, the theater was generally regarded as an extension of the Gay Quarters. Of course in Japan the Gay Quarters helped nourish literature and the arts. *Kabuki* was patronized by the *samurai*

[198]

and the nobility as well as by the townspeople. But these patrons themselves saw this activity as a purely private pleasure. For in the brothel or in the theater as well, a *samurai* was respected not for his social position, since such activities had nothing to do with the public order. Here only the connoisseur of his pleasure was admired. In the West, the Court and the theater were connected together and belonged to the same world; public and private life were not opposed. In Japan, however, the "public" court and the "private" theater constructed quite different worlds for themselves.

In the Meiji Period, however, the power of the public world increased tremendously. Efforts were made to mobilize all the resources that had previously gone into supporting all those "private" worlds, resources now to be used in the construction of a politically modern state. Therefore the sphere of culture was also divided in two. That culture which had long been identified as "public"—what was seen as "serious" culture—was given an enormous push. Such culture was represented precisely by the kind of school education and by the habits of reading I mentioned a moment ago. But the development of the theater fell far behind. It must be emphasized that such a moralistic point of view represented not merely a political strategem on the part of the government but actually reflected as well the general sentiments of the population at that time. The view was widely held that the first duty of the nation was to make herself as strong as possible. There was no room for doubt that the theater represented a purely private pleasure.

The movement to give the theater a connection with public culture and to make its efforts more "serious" in nature was carried on at the same time, and as a part, of the movement to "improve the drama." In order to give the theater a proper public image a plan was carried out to invite the Emperor himself to witness a *kabuki* perfor-

mance. And in order to make this new spectacle a more
"serious" one, dramas were written that remained quite
faithful to historical fact. However, in the first instance
the results obtained never permitted the theater to re-
place, or even to rival, the "seriousness" of printed matter. As for the second, the new dramas created were
merely boring to watch. By this time, reading had become the central fact of Japanese cultural life. The
phenomenon still continues today. Leaving out the question of mass-circulation magazines, popular everywhere,
Japan surely holds a special place among all the advanced
nations of the world in terms of the quantity of printed
material available. In any town you care to visit, look
into a large bookstore on a busy street: you will find
every evening huge piles of reading material piled about
on the large counters, like food in a market. As an
American reporter wrote recently in *The New York Times
Book Review,* "they don't sell greeting cards in Japanese
bookstores." Needless to say, all kinds of light reading
matter is sold, but the quantity of "serious" books
purchased is also high. About ten years ago, for example,
a Japanese publishing firm began issuing a series of
"great books of the world." More than four hundred
thousand copies of Nietzsche's *Also sprach Zarathustra*
were sold.

Such a set of circumstances certainly has an effect
on playwrights, even now. In my own case, my plays
printed in book form usually sell in the neighborhood of
ten thousand copies, yet usually not more than half that
number ever see a given play of mine in the theater.

Taking this situation as a background, the difficulties
in the development of the New Theater Movement since
the time of Osanai Kaoru [1881–1928] become easier to
understand. For the real and fundamental opposition to
the New Theater Movement came, not from an unfeeling

government nor from the rapid development of a tasteless popular theater, but from the public's fundamental longing for "serious" culture and education. On this point, Antoine in France took the boulevard theater for his enemy, just as later Eugene O'Neill was to see the Broadway of his day as his real opponent. The situation was much different in Japan: the Western serious theater attacked popular entertainment, but the New Theater in Japan had to wage war on a whole complex of attitudes about what was "serious," attitudes held by the whole population.

In order to confront such an implacable enemy the New Theater Movement was forced to arm itself with still another kind of "seriousness." From the beginning the movement sought to educate and to enlighten. Realism was stressed, and a preference for tragedy over comedy was established. At first such attitudes may show little accord with the sorts of ideas supported by the government. Yet, in terms of an educational goal leading to a modern way of life, certain resemblances become apparent.

Later, in the Taishō Period [1912–1926], and after, the New Theater Movement was strengthened in its political proclivities. The adoption of Marxist ideology was surely inevitable. Now, however, it seems clear that without battling the very concept of "seriousness" itself the theater could never hope to win the war against the habit of reading. For whatever the "serious" message of the theater might be, political or apolitical, its means of delivering that message could hardly be more efficient than that provided by written matter. Even putting aside the intellectual contents of the printed page, the reader will always take the act of reading more seriously than he will that of watching a play in the theater. Sitting quietly, at night, with a book spread open on the desk under a

[201]

lamp—even if the book is a novel—suggests an abstinence, a mood of contemplation far more strongly than does visiting a theater with family or friends.

From this point of view, the New Theater challenged an enemy it might never conquer. Those in the world of the New Theater who fought that hopeless battle were thus made to feel all the more isolated and alone. They learned all the more to strengthen the moralistic attitudes they had already taken. They tried to oppose the written word by making their dramas "intellectual," and they tried to oppose the ideals of education provided in the schools by insisting that society be cleansed. (As a related phenomenon, it might be mentioned that this "enlightening role" assumed by the New Theater Movement has had its effect on the popular commercial theater as well. The Takarazuka Girl Review, surely the most banefully typical example of Japanese popular entertainment, officially calls its actresses "pupils.") Eventually this high moral sense of the New Theater Movement, aided by a sense of isolation, began to move the theater not merely toward a position that supported a more perfect society but toward one that actually advocated political revolution. Marxism had a considerable effect on all aspects of life in the Taishō period, but nowhere were the results so pervasively felt as in the activities of the New Theater Movement. The blatant opposition of the movement to the morality of the establishment at that time was so much emphasized that, in artistic terms at least, the theater began to pursue a course fraught with danger.

TR: The politically active theater that began in the late 1920s and continued until World War II did much to color the spirit of the theater then and its influence could still be felt after the war as well. In the eyes of most Japanese critics, this political theater made many positive contributions. What would your own evaluation be?

YM: The greatest service rendered by the prewar political theater groups consisted in their formation of theatrical troupes to which the actors contributed funds, troupes that could manage to mount productions of plays not of a purely commercial nature. Even now the performers who earn money from films and television contribute a certain amount to their troupes for the presentation of artistically important plays. There are no actor's unions. The performers, without fees, play the roles assigned and may even go around to sell tickets to the audience. All such activities represent the good side of that high moral stance taken by the New Theater Movement. I fear, however, that such attitudes may not persist indefinitely.

Japanese Theater Now

TR: To me, as a foreign observer, the New Theater in Japan seems quite an "intellectual" theater. "Entertainment," even of the Broadway sort, is usually relegated to popular troupes with no "artistic" pretensions. Is such a division of value?

YM: Yes, the New Theater up until now has certainly been "intellectual" and "earnest," for reasons I explained above. Even should this attitude change in the future, that change will be slow in coming. The reason for this is that the theater (and here I include the purely commercial theater as well) plays a relatively small role in the conception of entertainment held by the Japanese public. Japan has no Broadway, nothing like American musicals, with their tremendously broad appeal. Ordinarily, general Japanese adult habits of entertainment no longer involve taking the whole family out in the evening. "Entertainment" means entertainment at home—reading a book or looking at television. These habits are reinforced in turn by current developments in urban construction patterns. City workers now live farther and farther from the center

[203]

of the city. Once home, they find it an imposition to return again to the city in the evening.

Those who support theater of any kind in Japan today are those who are likely to be very "serious" persons themselves. They are those who oppose the usual customs of society, those who come to the theater despite any desire they might have simply to enjoy their leisure. A theater supported by such an audience, at least at this juncture, will for better or for worse go right on being "serious."

TR: Playwrighting is, of course, only one aspect in the totality of the theater, but in a "serious" theater such as you describe it surely remains the central focus of the whole enterprise. Or so it seems to me. Thus the total value of a theatrical experience (if one might put it that way) is closely linked to the excellence of the drama being performed. Do you share my view?

YM: You are quite right. And the tensions involved might be suggested by an example from the Japanese theater. In the 1960s many young actors and directors tried to wage war on what they called the superiority of literature over the theater. They attempted to create an improvisatory theater, with a great emphasis on the physical role of the actor, and on accidental happenings. Yet during the same period Shinchōsha, one of the leading publishing firms in Japan, began putting out a series of new dramas by playwrights and novelists, independent of any support from the theater troupes.

TR: What prewar and postwar authors would you choose as representative in the development of a modern theater of literary accomplishment?

YM: Any examination of the history of the New Theater in Japan will begin with the names of two playwrights who wrote both modern dramas and *Kabuki* plays. They are Okamoto Kidō [1872–1939] and Mayama Seika [1878–1948]. Both tried to combine the theatricality of

[204]

traditional forms with the rational structures of modern drama. There are many, of course, who wrote plays with no reference whatsoever to older Japanese theatrical forms. Of those active in the prewar years, three names in particular might be cited: Kishida Kunio [1890–1954], Kubo Sakae [1901–1958], and Morimoto Kaoru [1912–1946]. Kishida was much influenced by such French dramatists as Jules Renard and Porto-Riche; Kubo wrote using the techniques of Socialist Realism; Morimoto was first stimulated by his reading of Noel Coward. All succeeded in creating theatrical characters appropriate to their times. Among postwar writers, one might first mention three whose work has already appeared in translation, Kinoshita Junji [b. 1914; *Yūzuru, Evening Crane*], Mishima Yukio [1925–1970]; *Sade kōshaku fujin, Madame de Sade*], and Abe Kōbō [b. 1924; *Tomodachi,* Friends]. The most important playwright whose work remains untranslated is Tanaka Chikao (born 1905). Tanaka blends his traditional Japanese sensibilities with Catholic belief; he stands as a kind of Japanese Mauriac. He shows in his work a wide variety of theatrical experimentation.

TR: Who are the younger writers whose work most bears watching? What plays in particular have impressed you?

YM: There are many names I might mention. Here are two. Yashiro Seiichi, the youngest disciple of Kinoshita Junji, is widely appreciated for his subtle poetic style in dialogue and for the sophisticated means by which he handles his rather heavy psychological subjects. I am thinking in particular of his play *Yoake ni kieta* (The One Who Vanished in the Dawn). Betsuyaku Minoru, who belongs to the youngest generation, is usually regarded as one of the "underground" playwrights. But as his first play *Matchiuri no Shōjo* (The Little Match Girl), eloquently testifies, he remains rather a poet of the theater, mixing humor and the grotesque.

[205]

An Interview with Yamazaki Masakazu

TR: Some critics have suggested that the new "underground" theater in Japan has taken away the creative energy from the New Theater. Do you agree?

YM: The greatest service performed by the so-called "underground" theater has been in undermining the narrow concept of realism maintained until now by the New Theater movement. These performers, rather than creating a monotonous copy of the gestures of everyday life or merely acting out explanations of the current social situation, appeal directly to the spectators' sense of theatrical possibility through their physical dynamism. Until now, realistic techniques have provided the strongest influence on our acting style; and I must admit as well that the techniques of non-realistic bodily expression available in such contemporary art forms as modern dance are as yet not well-established in Japan. Therefore the emergence of this new and extravagant impromptu style has given quite a shock to the New Theater. As a result, some insist the underground theater has brought a revolution. But I do not believe the vital destiny of our modern theater has been truly changed.

Why do I feel this way? In the first place, the obvious results suggested by such an impromptu acting still are easy to observe—a disregard for the dramatic text and a tendency to create an "anti-literary theater." Yet ironically, this improvisional art without a text slips easily into conventions of its own. Since the actor's body and brain cannot take the time on the stage to respond deeply to a given situation, the performer is therefore compelled to respond with habitual clichés. At first glance, the results may seem expressive, fresh and accidental; yet actually such expressiveness tends merely to repeat itself, since the actor only uses himself as a model.

I once had the opportunity to see the splendid New York production of Richard Shechner's *Dionysus 66*. I found it the very best of its kind. And yet, the experience taught me an important lesson. In the play, there are many occasions when the various actors are called on to create improvised conversations. They exchange trivialities about their everyday affairs and so create a free and lively impression. By accident, however, I happened to see the play on the day of the funeral of Robert Kennedy. One of the actors suddenly remembered the assassination. "Hey," he said, "what did you do yesterday at Bob's coffin?" Suddenly the actors lost all their suppleness. They stiffened. An awkward silence followed for several seconds. I suddenly realized that all of that self-generated "ordinary" conversation that seemed so fresh and natural was only possible as long as the actors were merely reacting to situations familiar to them, repeating their reactions by reflex. Faced with an unusual event—the murder of Robert Kennedy—the flow of their actions, codified by force of habit, was suddenly broken. The fact that they were really in a kind of stupor was suddenly clear.

A situation such as the death of Robert Kennedy is momentous; no ordinary words or gestures can convey the emotional confusion that everyone feels. In order to absorb the situation, then manifest it in words that carry fresh power, a certain time is required for the very choice of these words. A playwright can create such words quietly, in his study, choosing phrases and gestures appropriate to the situation. There are no doubt many reasons why the test is important in the theatre, but surely the most vital of them involves the ability to remove the real action of the play from mere stimulation and response. Unlike the animals, man has the special ability to respond to a given stimulus with a deliberated reaction. The drama functions to compress this reflex-like process of deliberation. To put it another way, the drama does

not merely serve to add "poetry" to the physical movements of the actors but rather acts so as to concentrate the
genuine human meaning of those actions.

Drama: Language, Literature

TR: Are contemporary readers in Japan prepared to consider
drama as literature? Because of the centrality of Shakespeare in our own English tradition, that assumption is
strong in English-speaking countries. But will Japanese
readers take a play as seriously as a poem or a novel?

YM: Japanese readers certainly enjoy all kinds of reading matter and are quite prepared to read the text of a play as
"literature." A play that is produced commercially
usually finds its way into print at the same time, usually
in a magazine or, in some cases, as a separate book. As I
mentioned a moment ago, Shinchōsha, one of the best-
known firms publishing in the literary field, began issuing a modern Japanese drama series. So far, more than
thirty-odd volumes have appeared. The most popular
dramatists read in translation are Shakespeare and Chekhov, but dramatists from Sophocles to Pinter are widely
appreciated. I also might add that it seems to me that as
the contemporary novel has become increasingly complex, the complaint that dramas are hard to read is less
and less meaningful.

TR: Does not the Japanese spoken language pose special
problems for the playwright? Spoken Japanese contains
perhaps more homonyms than any other language in the
world. A survey of world languages indicated that Japanese has a very low "mutual comprehensibility rate";
two speakers of Japanese may understand only, say 80%
of what they say to each other, while for English the rate
is something like 94%.

An Interview with Yamazaki Masakazu

YM: I certainly agree that the problem of the Japanese language—that is, of Japanese as a spoken language—is an important one. Yet I don't think the most serious difficulties lie in the area of homonyms and resulting problems of mutual comprehensibility. I think that between Japanese the verbal context usually provides sufficient information for clarity. I don't believe those difficulties are there.

TR: Nevertheless, I can't help but suspect that the use of dialogue involving the use of many words using Chinese compound characters may make difficulties for the auditor in the theater. Certainly I have heard formal addresses in Japan which, although they might be clear enough if the eye could see the written characters, remain ambiguous to the ear. And even on television newscasts one notices that written characters are often provided while the announcer speaks, presumably to avoid this sort of ambiguity.

Let me choose a more specific example, a line early in the opening scene of *Sanetomo*. The line, which describes Sanetomo's rank, sounds clear enough in English because many of the words are polysyllabic.

"Great Manor Lord of Japan, General Warden. Third Kamakura Shōgun, Chief Commander of the Warriors. Lord Minamoto Sanetomo."

Here is the line (romanized) in Japanese:

"Nihon koku sōjitō sōshugo. Kamakura bakufu sandai no shōgun. Buke no tōryō, Minamoto Sanetomo."

With the speed at which such a line must be pronounced, I wonder if such words as *"sōjitō sōshugo"* or *"tōryō"* can really be caught and properly digested in the theater. To the eye the meaning is clear, from the Chinese characters. But for the ear? I wonder.

YM: I cannot deny that homonyms cause a great deal of trouble for the comprehensibility of spoken Japanese, if the playwright is careless. But such difficulties can be kept to

[209]

a minimum. In the case you mention, for example, the word *tōryō* (a chief) is a word easily understood orally, through its frequent use in such expressions as *daiku no tōryō* (a chief carpenter). I must admit that both *sōjitō* and *sōshugo* may be a bit hard for, say, a high school graduate to understand. Yet even so the prefix *sō-* is quickly grasped through its use in such compounds as *sōryō* (the eldest son), *sōdaishō* (a leading general), or *sōtō* (the Fuhrer). In all cases, the suggestion is of something that is the leading, the greatest. Therefore, even if *-jitō* or *-shugo* should be difficult to comprehend for some of the audience, the association with *sō-* will help them to understand that Sanetomo is, in some sense, a leading personage in Japan at the time.

TR: For you, then, where do the serious problems lie?

TM: I believe that the real difficulties lie in the great difference in Japanese between the spoken and written languages. Unlike the European languages, and unlike Chinese, the forces of grammatical control are rather weak in Japanese. Therefore if the proper verbal tension is not maintained in the course of a conversation, there is a real danger of linguistic slippage, even collapse. In ordinary daily conversation compound sentences have a tendency to collapse into simple sentences; and in compound sentences the relation between subjects and objects often become ambiguous, In a conversation between two persons, they will, of course, have no trouble understanding each other. Yet a third party standing listening to them will have great difficulty in following what is said. And of course, in a play, the spectator represents this "third party." Even in a realistic play dialogue must be created which the spectator can understand. The actor, of course, must discipline himself so as to produce his words with the utmost clarity possible; yet even those words must be arranged with a grammatical precision that pushes them closer to the written lan-

[210]

guage. And because there is such a great discrepancy between this language and the language of ordinary
conversation, such stage language may well strike the
auditors in the theater as "artificial" or "affected."

TR: Ironically, why is it that some of these same speeches that
sound so "stilted," at least to me, seem so reasonable and
effective when translated into a Western language?

TM: I think that when such speech or dialogue is translated
into a Western language, the results are bound to sound
more natural, since even ordinary conversation in Western languages is far closer to the written language than in
Japanese. In my own case, I very much enjoy my plays
when they are translated into other languages, and precisely because of this very problem. In a play, of course,
there must always exist a certain contradiction between
the style of the author's literary text and the actuality of
the spoken dialogue.

TR: In your own view, what are the current developments in
Japanese drama viewed as literature? Is the future a
bright one?

YM: I believe that the present situation in the theater—and its
future problems—remain about the same both in Japan
and in the West. Since the end of the Second World War
the theater has shown an intense concern for problems of
methodology and technique, ranging from the "theater of
the absurd" to the "anti-literary theater" of the 1960s.
Playwrights and directors alike have presented their productions as actual demonstrations of dramatic theory. Yet
by the early 1970s this fever had passed and there
seemed to be a general sense of a loss of direction. I hesitate to make any predictions, but I do think it is clear to
many that the "theater of the absurd" or the "anti-literary theater" merely represents two possible approaches among many. When that point is finally
grasped by everyone concerned then, I think, we will see
a new age of drama beginning.

[211]

An Interview with Yamazaki Masakazu

TR: One last question on the subject of drama as literature. Do you believe that the Japanese who read drama as literature make any fundamentally differing evaluation of modern Japanese dramatists than do those who form their opinions from stage performances? Will a "literary" evaluation of the history of the New Theater Movement differ in any essential way from a "theatrical" evaluation?

YM: There are variations, certainly. Yet in the end I think that there is no fundamental difference between these two means of evaluation.

TR: To an American observer, at least, the custom of the Japanese theatrical troupe seems quite different from our own director-producer system. Indeed, it seems rather difficult to imagine all the advantages and disadvantages of a system so different from our own.

YM: The greatest advantage of the company system lies in the fidelity and devotion of the actors: through their efforts, plays that are not merely commercial in nature can thus be produced. By the same token, the greatest danger of such a system lies in the possibility that the maintenance of such troupes may come to represent the only purpose of such efforts, thus creating in effect a sort of commercial theater troupe.

TR: Again, to a foreign observer it seems that the relationship between the desire to introduce foreign drama and the wish to develop a genuine contemporary Japanese drama by producing new plays may produce some confusions or contradictions in the policies of the theater companies. At the least, it seems that the purposes are not quite the same. Does this dual function produce any contradictions?

YM: The selection of plays to be presented always presents a problem: all over the world the same few famous plays are mounted again and again. I don't think, however, that the Japanese troupes show any difference in their policies for selecting Japanese and Western plays for production. Such a distinction does not now represent an important one; rather, it indicates differences in the tastes of the writers and directors of the various troupes involved.

TR: How do theater companies recognize and encourage young playwrights? Does such encouragement represent the surest way for a young playwright to become known? Are there other ways?

YM: The theater companies play a role, certainly, but the importance of the drama magazines must not be overlooked either. There are three such magazines, plus some literary magazines as well, that provide opportunities for young playwrights to publish their work. Such publication in turn gives these young writers more opportunities to attract the attention of the theater troupes. One magazine gives a yearly drama prize, named after Kishida Kunio, to the best new playwright of the year. That prize often guarantees his future.

TR: It seems to me that revivals of earlier modern Japanese plays are relatively rare. How do Japanese audiences learn about their own New Theater tradition? In New York, for example, we can usually see productions of Wilder, O'Neill, early Williams, etc., to say nothing of the classics—Shakespeare, Chekhov, etc.

TM: It is true that revivals of older modern Japanese plays are few. The New Theater Movement has used its energies to move forward, to renew itself; any desire to assess past experience has therefore been weakened. The New Theater movement sees its real traditions in the Western classics: the plays of Shakespeare, Molière, and Chekhov are revived constantly in Japan. On one side are those Western classics; on the other, the classical *nō* and *kabuki*. The New Theater does not think in terms of creating "classics."

[213]

An Interview with Yamazaki Masakazu

TR: But it is just at this point that I hope you might for a moment abandon your role as a practicing playwright to look at the situation from your point of view as a literary critic. It seems to me that there has been a certain failure, on the part of the New Theater Movement, to identify and study those modern Japanese dramatic texts which might, if nothing else, serve as models and examples for, say, the proper writing of dialogue (such a difficult business, as we discussed earlier), construction of plot, and so forth. And this is to say nothing of the plays that capture the whole intellectual and emotional thrust of a generation, the place a play like *Otto to yobareru Nihonjin* (A Japanese Called Otto) of Kinoshita Junji seems to me to occupy, for example. I myself cannot help but feel that as long as the New Theater continues to look for its inspiration to foreign models, it will not escape a certain artificiality. Surely, from a literary point of view in any case, there now exists a body of drama written since about 1900 from which one may select and identify works of real artistic merit. Should not the theater troupes take the lead in identifying and reviving such works?

YM: I agree with you one hundred per cent. I have nothing to add to what you have said, and indeed, as a man of the theater myself, I feel an obligation to take some initiatives in that direction.

TR: Well then, in your role as literary critic what eight or ten plays might you choose that best represent the tradition, plays that might even be revived and give pleasure now?

YM: Here are a few suggestions, for a start: Kishida Kunio: *Chiroru no aki* (Autumn in the Tyrols), *Kamifusen* (Paper Balloon), *Sawa-shi no futari musume* (Mr. Sawa's Two Daughters) Kinoshita Junji: *Twilight Crane, A Japanese Named Otto* Tanaka Chikao: *Kyōiku* (Education), *Maria no kubi* (The Head of the Madonna), *Hizen fukoki* (*A Description of Hizen*) Mishima Yukio: modern *nō* drama.

[214]

An Interview with Yamazaki Masakazu

TR: A few questions about audiences. Do they tend to see only the work of one company, or do they watch the efforts of various troupes? To what extent do devotees of the modern theater attend *nō* and *kabuki* performances as well? And have audiences learned to enjoy themselves at the theater, or do they still regard the experience of watching a modern drama as a "learning" experience?

YM: It certainly used to be the case that the New Theater productions were largely supported by audiences recruited from various organizations—labor unions, social organizations, and so forth. Since the 1960s, however, the power of such groups has weakened. Audiences that support only one troupe have dwindled, and audiences that only attend productions of the modern theater have shrunk as well. Recently, for example, there was a tremendously successful production of *Macbeth* given in Tokyo. In that production, Lady Macbeth was played by Bandō Tamasaburō, a well-known actor of female roles from *kabuki*. Certainly our present conception of the "New Theater" will not vanish overnight, but I think that as various elements evolve the movement will grow increasingly diversified and that, at the same time, our formerly narrow "moral spirit" will be broadened as well. Certainly the "New Theater" will continue to be a serious one: but at least this "seriousness" will come more and more to reflect the sympathies and excitement felt by its audiences.

Modern Asian Literature Series

Neo-Confucian Studies

Translations From the Oriental Classics

Records of the Grand Historian of China, translated from the Shih chi of Ssu-ma Ch'ien, tr. Burton Watson, 2 vols.   1961

Instructions for Practical Living and Other Neo-Confucian Writings by Wang Yang-ming, tr. Wing-tsit Chan   1963

Chuang Tzu: Basic Writings, tr. Burton Watson, paperback ed. only   1964

The Mahābhārata, tr. Chakravarthi V. Narasimhan. Also in paperback ed.   1965

The Manyōshū, Nippon Gakujutsu Shinkōkai edition   1965

Su Tung-p'o: Selections from a Sung Dynasty Poet, tr. Burton Watson. Also in paperback ed.   1965

Bhartrihari: Poems, tr. Barbara Stoler Miller. Also in paperback ed.   1967

Basic Writings of Mo Tzu, Hsün Tzu, and Han Fei Tzu, tr. Burton Watson. Also in separate paperback eds.   1967

The Awakening of Faith, Attributed to Aśvaghosha, tr. Yoshito S. Hakeda. Also in paperback ed.   1967

Reflections on Things at Hand: The Neo-Confucian Anthology, comp. Chu Hsi and Lü Tsu-ch'ien, tr. Wing-tsit Chan   1967

The Platform Sutra of the Sixth Patriarch, tr. Philip B. Yampolsky. Also in paperback ed.   1967

Essays in Idleness: The Tsurezuregusa of Kenkō, tr. Donald Keene. Also in paperback ed.   1967

The Pillow Book of Sei Shōnagon, tr. Ivan Morris, 2 vols.   1967

Two Plays of Ancient India: The Little Clay Cart and the Minister's Seal, tr. J. A. B. van Buitenen   1968

The Complete Works of Chuang Tzu, tr. Burton Watson   1968

The Romance of the Western Chamber (Hsi Hsiang chi), tr. S. I. Hsiung. Also in paperback ed.   1968

The Manyōshū, Nippon Gakujutsu Shinkōkai edition. Paperback text edition.   1969

Records of the Historian: Chapters from the Shih chi of Ssu-ma Ch'ien. Paperback text edition, tr. Burton Watson   1969

Cold Mountain: 100 Poems by the T'ang Poet Han-shan, tr. Burton Watson. Also in paperback ed.   1970

Twenty Plays of the Nō Theatre, ed. Donald Keene. Also in paperback ed.   1970

Chūshingura: The Treasury of Loyal Retainers, tr. Donald Keene. Also in paperback ed.   1971

Studies in Oriental Culture

[219]

2. *Chinese Government in Ming Times: Seven Studies,* ed. Charles O. Hucker — 1969
3. *The Actors' Analects (Yakusha Rongo),* ed. and tr. by Charles J. Dunn and Bunzō Torigoe — 1969
4. *Self and Society in Ming Thought,* by Wm. Theodore de Bary and the Conference on Ming Thought. Also in paperback ed. — 1970
5. *A History of Islamic Philosophy,* by Majid Fakhry — 1970
6. *Phantasies of a Love Thief: The Caurapancāśikā Attributed to Bilhaṇa,* by Barbara Stoler Miller — 1971
7. *Iqbal: Poet-Philosopher of Pakistan,* ed. Hafeez Malik — 1971
8. *The Golden Tradition: An Anthology of Urdu Poetry,* by Ahmed Ali. Also in paperback ed. — 1973
9. *Conquerors and Confucians: Aspects of Political Change in Late Yüan China,* by John W. Dardess — 1973
10. *The Unfolding of Neo-Confucianism,* by Wm. Theodore de Bary and the Conference on Seventeenth-Century Chinese Thought. Also in paperback ed. — 1975
11. *To Acquire Wisdom: The Way of Wang Yang-ming,* by Julia Ching — 1976
12. *Gods, Priests, and Warriors: The Bhṛgus of the Mahābhārata,* by Robert P. Goldman — 1977
13. *Mei Yao-ch'en and the Development of Early Sung Poetry,* by Jonathan Chaves — 1976
14. *The Legend of Semimaru, Blind Musician of Japan,* by Susan Matisoff — 1977

Companions to Asian Studies

Approaches to the Oriental Classics, ed. Wm. Theodore de Bary — 1959
Early Chinese Literature, by Burton Watson. Also in paperback ed. — 1962
Approaches to Asian Civilizations, ed. Wm. Theodore de Bary and Ainslie T. Embree — 1964
The Classic Chinese Novel: A Critical Introduction, by C. T. Hsia. Also in paperback ed. — 1968

[220]

Chinese Lyricism: Shih Poetry from the Second to the Twelfth Century, tr. Burton Watson. Also in paperback ed.   1971

A Syllabus of Indian Civilization, by Leonard A. Gordon and Barbara Stoler Miller   1971

Twentieth-Century Chinese Stories, ed. C. T. Hsia and Joseph S. M. Lau. Also in paperback ed.   1971

A Syllabus of Chinese Civilization, by J. Mason Gentzler, 2d ed.   1972

A Syllabus of Japanese Civilization, by H. Paul Varley, 2d ed.   1972

An Introduction to Chinese Civilization, ed. John Meskill, with the assistance of J. Mason Gentzler   1973

An Introduction to Japanese Civilization, ed. Arthur E. Tiedemann   1974

A Guide to Oriental Classics, ed. Wm. Theodore de Bary and Ainslie T. Embree, 2d ed. Also in paperback ed.   1975

Introduction to Oriental Civilizations
Wm. Theodore de Bary, *Editor*

Sources of Japanese Tradition	1958	Paperback ed., 2 vols.	1964
Sources of Indian Tradition	1958	Paperback ed., 2 vols.	1964
Sources of Chinese Tradition	1960	Paperback ed., 2 vols.	1964